Kindness and Respect

Kindness and Respect

An Experiential Approach to
Social-Emotional Learning

Charlie Richardson

with

Jess Anderson and **Lisa Steele-Maley**
Illustrations by **Phyllis Sabattis**

Kindness and Respect
2020 © Kieve Wavus Education, Inc.
ISBN 978-0-578-71563-6

Cover Artist: Debbie Loughlin
Copy Editor and Proofreader: Amy Stackhouse
Book and Cover Designer: Lindy Gifford
Published by Kieve Wavus Education, Inc.
Printed by Penmor Lithographers, Lewiston, Maine

Dedicated to the memory of Richard C. (Dick) Kennedy,
who taught that all young people are at promise
and that we do the greatest good when we teach the teachers.
Thank you, Dick.
Now it is our turn to pass it on.

Preface

Kindness and Respect is a collection of practical, proven activities for building a healthy, resilient, and engaged community of learners. If this book has found its way to you, you are likely an educator or administrator who is looking for ways to build a healthier learning environment while better supporting individual participants. You know that individuals learn best in an environment that supports them emotionally and socially as well as physically and intellectually. We know that your time and energy are limited and that there are dozens of demands on you. That's before you even count the number of participants in your program, classroom, or school! As an educator and administrator, I know that it takes time and energy to construct a positive learning environment. I also know that it is worth it.

In the early 1980s, I was invited to the shores of Damariscotta Lake to work a six-week pilot program at Camp Kieve. In one-week sessions, participants from six Maine schools lived and learned together in safe, healthy, and eye-opening ways. Confidence and aspirations rose as participants expanded their horizons by trying new things, working together, and making healthy decisions. As participants departed at the end of each week, they left with an expanded sense of themselves and a deeper understanding of how they could meaningfully pursue their dreams. As I departed at the end of the six weeks, I left with a clear sense of direction for my own life.

Now, 30 years later, I have worked at a handful of public and private schools, returning almost annually to the camp on the lake. In every role in every institution, I have leaned into experiences and activities from camp to meet both participants and staff members as whole individuals. I am convinced that, by addressing social, emotional, physical, and spiritual needs and goals as well as intellectual ones, I have been a more effective history teacher, adviser, dean of students, coach, dorm parent, and parent.

The world has changed a lot since I began working with young people, but much remains the same. Kindness and respect are still foundational building blocks for any relationship. Verbal and nonverbal communication operate on the same two-way street. Our community is stronger when we respect our differences and honor our similarities.

These guiding principles, and more, are foundations at Kieve Wavus Education. The program that I started with has grown into a cornerstone of the organization. The Leadership School and Educator in Residence programs serve thousands of young people from scores of communities each year. Every day we are fortunate to hear two types of success stories from our school-based programs. One is the story of the individual—the participant who conquers a fear, finds a strong voice, sets a new goal, or makes a new friend. The other is the story of the community—the people who share schools and classrooms all year long yet don't always see one another clearly until they are brought together to face common challenges with laughter and gentle guidance, and to break down barriers with common language and actions, guided always by respect and kindness for one another. We see the profound impact of our work one participant, one teacher, one school, and one community at a time.

At a time when testing, technology, and school safety dominate conversations about education, it may seem a little odd for a nearly 100-year-old summer camp to offer a book of curriculum and methodology to schools. School invokes images of desks and papers, chairs and bells, lockers and hallways. Summer camp invokes images of campfires and games, swimming and sunsets. It makes sense that these images are different. Schools and camps have different roles to play in the lives of young people. They are, however, very compatible. They share the common goal of supporting young people in meeting their potential.

In service to that shared goal, we gladly offer this book to you. May it serve as guidance and inspiration for you and your colleagues as you seek ways to nurture whole, healthy individuals in a positive, productive school community.

Charlie Richardson
KWE Director of Education

Acknowledgments

It is said that we stand on the shoulders of those who have come before us. That feels especially true at Kieve Wavus Education. Here, Kennedy family leadership is approaching its fourth generation, and participants are immersed in experiences that their parents and grandparents can remember fondly. From 1985 to 2001, Charlie and Wendy Harrington developed a clear vision for the Leadership School and nurtured it with commitment, hard work, and creativity. Through those years, Jim Grout offered professional development and guidance that still serve us now.

Each generation and each individual leaves a mark, a legacy. As experiential educators, we must be adept at embracing these lingering legacies and adapting them to enhance our ongoing programming. We cannot name every individual who has contributed to the work that is captured here, but we appreciate the teaching, mentoring, and inspiration from all of them.

The field of experiential learning is highly collaborative and constantly evolving. Our daily work and this book benefit from the thousands of counselors, educators, and administrators who have passed through Kieve Wavus Education (KWE) over the past 100 years. Their contributions of time, creativity, energy, and commitment have shaped, refined, and re-refined our curriculum and approach to best meet the needs of the young people we serve. Some of the activities in this book are "originals"—activities developed here at KWE to meet the specific needs and goals of our participants. While we can no longer pinpoint the creators, we are indebted to them.

While a number of activities and concepts in this book are similar to those used by other outdoor and adventure education providers, our approach is unique and has been refined over years of use by dozens of facilitators. We are grateful to be able to continually learn and grow alongside an increasing number of excellent outdoor education and adventure education organizations as well as the schools we serve. Our collaborations and sharing in books, trainings, and workshops have helped us each to develop the best possible programs for our constituents over the years.

Lastly, we are thankful for the participants, who honor us with their trust and their wisdom. Every day, they encourage us to be the most creative, adaptable, and encouraging mentors, educators, and citizens we can be.

Contents

Introduction

The emerging interest in addressing social-emotional learning (SEL) is more than a passing phase. It is an invitation to schools to reorient their values, structures, and curriculum toward optimal human development. It is an opportunity for schools to pay close attention to the ways in which school culture and climate support or dampen learning for all students. It is an invitation for the American education system to step into its responsibility to support young people in developing the skills and competencies they will need as they enter adulthood in an increasingly complex and volatile world.

While incorporating explicit SEL curriculum into the classroom is new for many schools, it has always been inherent in our work. While teaching classes called Skills, Decisions, Relationships, Teambuilding, and Adventure, KWE educators guide SEL skill building through experiential learning. As we work with schools year after year, we see firsthand how their communities grow and change over time. We have seen how our approach not only builds individual SEL competencies but also strengthens communities—and we have seen how hard it is for schools to incorporate this work amid other institutional priorities.

We have also seen that while it is hard, it is not impossible. Teachers and administrators are resourceful and creative. They find ways to coach healthy communication while simultaneously teaching long division. They find ways to foster participant decision making while exploring choices made by world leaders. They find ways to build community and honor individual differences while discussing literature. And we know they will find ways to integrate the activities and approaches offered in this book into their classrooms and schools.

The Experiential Cycle

Experiential learning is learning by doing. It is traditionally described as a four-step cycle. Engaging participants in interesting activities and experiences (**Experience**) is only one part of that cycle. While it may be the most obvious and the most fun, it is only the first step. Providing participants with time to think about what they have done (**Reflect**) and reserving the time to talk about the experience (**Process**) are both necessary. Reflection and processing help participants arrive at the point where they can generalize their learning and apply it to future experiences (**Apply**). It is a rare person who

3

can pull the deepest level of learning from an activity or experience without taking time to reflect and process the experience.

Young people need to learn, practice, and apply SEL skills in the same way that they learn academic skills: through scaffolded instruction and practice both inside and outside of the classroom. We use an experiential model to teach SEL skills by creating teachable moments and encouraging reflection on those moments to process together what was successful and what was not. Facilitators create space for participants to engage in the process of effective communication, build relationships, practice decision making, collaborate, reflect, process, and adapt.

Getting Started: LEADSTAR

At Kieve Wavus Education, we believe that communication is the glue that holds relationships together. Without it, everything can fall apart. To set the tone for a successful and productive day, our first class is focused on communication skills. The "Eight Guidelines to Clear and Effective Communication"—LEADSTAR—set our foundation. The acronym is split into two parts: LEAD describes good listening, while STAR focuses on the speaker's responsibilities.

Listen to the entire message

Eye contact

Avoid distractions (and being a distraction)

Don't interrupt

Speak loudly and clearly

Think before you speak and act

Ask questions about the topic

Repeat the message

These eight guidelines for communication are fundamental to most of the activities in this book. LEADSTAR is the bedrock for the social-emotional understanding of ourselves, our communities, and our world.

You can introduce and reinforce the eight guidelines through a round of Simon Says that assigns a different gesture to each guideline. Remind participants to listen by placing your hands alongside your earlobes to extend them. Pointing at your eyes is a simple reminder to make eye contact. To represent avoiding distraction, create blinders with your hands positioned alongside your temples. Covering your mouth with your hand cues to not interrupt.

For speaking loudly and clearly, pretend to talk through a megaphone by creating a tube with your hands in front of your mouth. Tap your temple with one finger to remind participants to think before they speak and act. Raise your hand to cue participants to ask questions about the topic. Repeat the message by making your fingers move like wheels spinning in the mud.

As you think about how to teach and support developing communication skills, consider the dynamics of your group. Are they better at listening or speaking? Which of the components is the most challenging for them? Which is a strength?

Try some of these activities to assess and practice LEADSTAR:

Three-Step Directions: Offer a three-step direction. For instance, stand up, push in your chair, and put your finger on your nose. Wait. Is everyone able to follow the directions? If not, where do they get stuck? Are they distracted? Are they aware that they didn't hear the whole message? If listening is a challenge, try an activity like The Wright Family (p. 78) or Xerox (p. 84) to practice listening.

Eyes Up: Ask participants to stand in a circle so they can all see each other. Stand outside the circle to give instructions. When you say "Eyes up," everyone looks up and makes eye contact with another member of the circle. If the same person is looking back at them, the pair leaves the circle. If they have not made a match, they remain. As pairs leave the circle, have them work on a partner task such as a Partner Interview (p. 178). Are all participants comfortable with eye contact? While making eye contact demonstrates respect in mainstream American culture, some individuals and some cultures do not feel the same way. Explore cultural differences in nonverbal behavior like eye contact and discuss other ways that people demonstrate that they are listening to the speaker.

Delayed Follow the Leader: Start with a round of Follow the Leader. Do a movement and ask participants to copy it immediately. In Round 2, ask participants to wait until you have switched to the next movement to demonstrate the prior one. If they are successful, delay the movement they demonstrate to even earlier in the sequence. Similarly, ask participants to remember and repeat a clapping pattern back to see how many items in a sequence they can remember. Do they struggle to remember the sequence? Why? Are they distracted, or is this a cognitive challenge?

Hold It: Ask participants to summarize a story you have just read or the lesson you demonstrated aloud with each participant taking turns explaining it in sequence. When a participant is ready to share, ask them to take their turn by saying "Hold it" and challenge the sharing to stay connected like a string is running through it. For groups that struggle with interruption in any setting, use a talking piece or object. Only the participant with the talking piece can talk, and they must pass it to the next person when they are ready. If a group struggles to have group discussions, begin with partner activities like Mirror, Mirror (p. 22) or Paper Airplanes (p. 120) before moving to small groups and finally larger group discussions. Navigating a conversation in a large group often requires development of prerequisite skills.

Telephone: Participants pass a message by whispering to each other in sequence. Does the final participant receive the same message that the first participant heard? This activity, of course, is about listening and not about speaking loudly; however, it also highlights the need to speak clearly. Many of the team challenges in this book require participants to speak loudly and clearly in order to be successful. If participants struggle with speaking in large groups, start with pairs. If they have trouble being clear, practice some tongue twisters. If they struggle to speak at an appropriate volume, introduce a gesture to remind participants to raise their voices so they can be heard. You could also practice repeating the message by playing Telephone and asking participants to summarize oral or written course content as the first link in the chain. You might discuss what information is important to keep in order to send the same message or what you need to change to make the message your own.

Gotcha: Participants stand in a circle and put their right hands out to their sides, like they are holding a tray, and their left pointer finger just touching their neighbor's open palm. Decide on a magic word. If you say the magic word while telling a story, participants try to capture their neighbor's left finger without letting their own finger be captured. When the magic word has not been spoken, they should not be moving. This activity requires competency in more than one element of LEADSTAR to be successful, but it often encourages a conversation about thinking before acting. How much information do participants need before making decisions? For more advanced groups, Peanut Butter and Jelly Sandwich (p. 67) can highlight the importance of thinking before speaking (while also making everyone laugh).

20 Questions: Think of an object (an accessory like an umbrella or a specific animal are favorites) and challenge the participants to figure out the object by asking fewer than twenty yes-or-no questions. After participants are comfortable asking questions, begin to offer more open-ended challenges that require them to stay focused on a particular topic, such as Mirage (p. 135) or Community Maps (p. 132).

Copycat: Choose one participant to be the guesser, and have them leave the room. When they are gone, choose a leader. The leader makes a movement that everyone copies. As soon as everyone copies, the leader makes another movement, and so on. The guesser returns to the group with the task of discovering the leader. This activity can initiate a conversation about the source of information.

How to Use This Book

For the sake of organization, the activities in this book have been sorted into five social-emotional competencies and sequenced based on increasing challenge level. However, this is not intended to be just another activity guide. It is meant to be a resource for inspiring active learning and reflection. Consider each activity as a starting point for the learning that will encourage participant social-emotional development and engagement and improve school culture and climate. Some of that learning will be made clear in the processing activities and conversations that help students integrate new awareness and experience into their daily lives. Some of the participant learning and growth will take place hours, days, weeks, or even years later as a participant recalls a comment or question or recognizes a new application for the experience in their own life.

Most of these activities have been designed with middle school students in mind. However, many of them have been used with participants of all ages, from first graders to adults. By modifying elements, language, the processing approach, or a combination, each activity can be tailored to meet the maturity level of your group. Sometimes an individual or group will need to struggle and fall short of a goal in order to learn and grow, but keep in mind that you will all have more fun and glean the most benefit from an activity if it is sufficiently challenging but not impossible. Additionally, by modifying the processing questions and reshaping the conversation after a particular activity, many of the activities presented here can be adapted to meet several competencies. For example, a self-awareness activity can become a self-management activity when you focus the processing and reflection on how the participants managed themselves instead of what they learned about themselves.

Each section begins with a relevant vignette from KWE programming followed by a brief description of that section's SEL competency. The activities in each section are presented in an appropriate sequence for guiding your participants into more complicated and more evocative learning. However, you will want to identify the entry point and adapt the sequence of activities to meet the readiness, needs, and goals of your group.

Each activity summary includes three parts: a warm-up, the main activity, and processing questions. There is further information about processing in the back of the book. Many of the warm-up and processing strategies can be mixed and matched with other activities. Activities can and should be adapted to meet your participants' needs, interests, and capacities. Some activities include examples of ways in which the activity can be connected to or adapted to academic content. These examples are intended to stimulate your creative application of the activities and questions in your setting. Customize them for your audience, setting, and group goals to make them your own. Some activities include facilitation tips—words of caution or guidance offered by KWE educators.

This is what we call the activity. You can rename it or may already know it by another name

Name Tags

Primary competency

SEL Competency: Social Awareness

What the participants will learn from the activity from the facilitator's perspective

Objectives

- Participants will practice strategies for building relationships with people who are different from themselves.
- Participants will recognize that other people may experience situations differently from themselves.
- Participants will recognize individual differences.

What you need to have on hand

Materials: Name tags and markers

Approximate time for the lesson from warm-up through processing

Time: 15–20 minutes

Introduces the lesson and sets the tone

Warm-Up: Ask participants to form a Perfect Circle. In a Perfect Circle, everyone is standing in alphabetical order by first name. For more challenge, ask them to do it without talking.

Step-by-step process

Procedure

1. Ask participants to write their names in the middle of a name tag.
2. Ask them to respond to a name tag question by writing the answer above their name.
3. Participants stand or sit in a circle and share their names and responses to the question.
4. Write the responses, without names, on the easel pad/whiteboard while they are shared.

Additional info

Use these name tag questions or make up your own

1. If you could fill an Olympic-sized swimming pool with anything, what would it be?

2. If you could have one song play every time you entered a room, what would it be?

3. If you could have any animal sit on your shoulder at all times, what would it be?

4. If you could combine two animals to make a new one, what two animals would you combine?

5. If you could have lunch with any person, dead or alive, who would it be?

6. If they made a movie about your life, who would play you?

Discussion questions to help participants reflect and generalize so they can apply what they've learned

Processing

1. What commonalities did you hear while participants were sharing? What differences?

2. Other than doing this activity, what is another way to learn more about your peers?

3. Find a partner and spend 2 minutes interviewing each other to find at least two things that you have in common. (See Partner Interview, p. 178.)

Ways to incorporate or integrate the activity into core academic content areas

 ## Connections to Content

Language Arts: Use the brainstorm to lead into a written reflection in response to the name tag question.

Lessons learned by experience

Facilitation Tip: Perfect Circle, Name Tags, and Partner Interview can all be reused as part of a classroom routine.

Competencies & Activities

Self-Awareness

Our first day was full of different activities that I thought were just games, but at the end of each activity, we sat down with our educator and talked about what it meant. We started the day by creating a Full Value Contract, in which we shared goals that we wished to accomplish by the end of the week as well as the values and skills we brought to our team. I had trouble thinking of what I was good at. We made rules for our group interactions and how we would each play a part in our team's success. I shared that I wanted everyone to listen to each other without interrupting. Later, we applied these goals and skills to all of the activities we were doing, and I learned I was good at helping my teammates, especially when they were frustrated. Throughout the day, we checked in with our group rules and goals to see how we were growing as individuals and as a team.

At the indoor climbing wall, we learned how to rock climb. Our educators introduced us to the concept of comfort zones and taught us how to safely belay and climb. I was a little nervous about the height of the wall and even more nervous about having to rely on my peers at the other end of the rope. As the week went on, I got to know my group better and we became a team. I was much more comfortable with the idea of being supported by five of my classmates. Their support, both physically and emotionally, gave me the courage I needed to push myself to the top of the wall and ring the bell. I was still feeling exhilaration when I finished our climbing session. Our educator had us identify the emotions we felt during our climbing block using cards that showed different feelings through pictures. I chose "accomplished."

At the end of the day, our group went into the woods for what our educator called solo time. We were asked to find our own space and be still, silent, and alone. At first, I thought I would be bored, but as time went on, I realized that I didn't usually get this level of alone time at home. I began to relax, rest, and reflect on my day and what I had learned about myself. While I was out there, I filled out a worksheet to think about my personal goals and different ways I could accomplish them. I learned to appreciate solo time and at the end of the week I wrote a letter to myself detailing everything I had learned about myself at Kieve Wavus Education.

This participant clearly describes their thoughts, emotions, and values throughout the experience. They verbalize that they had trouble identifying their strengths and were nervous, especially at the climbing wall. They use new vocabulary like "comfort zones" and "solo time." They articulate some of their struggles demonstrating a growth mind-set. They explain how the facilitator helped them establish individual and group goals. The facilitator promoted social-emotional learning through framing, activities, and reflection. By processing along the way, the participant received feedback that helped them learn to monitor and adjust their emotions and behavior.

Self-awareness is about recognizing how emotions, thoughts, values, and understanding affect behavior. It also includes accurately assessing one's strengths and weaknesses, ideally with well-grounded self-confidence, optimism, and a growth mind-set. Participants with strong self-awareness skills can figure out what they need to do to complete a task and are more resilient and willing to learn from their mistakes.

The activities in this section develop different skills and perspectives that contribute to increasing self-awareness. The first four activities encourage participants to explore emotions and practice a growth mind-set, viewing their abilities as malleable. The next group of activities challenge participants to become aware of their own perspectives and the ways in which they see and contribute to the world around them. The final three activities, How Did We Do Bingo, Tap Someone Who, and Letter to Self, are much more reflective than the others; they will be most effective after participants have completed at least two or three other activities. You can also adapt the last three activities to review academic content or reflect on an academic experience.

Card Prediction

SEL Competency: Self-Awareness

Objectives

- Participants will identify what triggers their emotions.
- Participants will use self-reflection to determine if their emotions and feelings are proportional to the situation.
- Participants will recognize how different emotions feel in their body.
- Participants will practice having a growth mind-set.

Materials: A deck of playing cards, paper, and pens/pencils

Time: 30 minutes

Warm-Up: Using Feelings Cards (p. 198) or by writing a word bank of emotions on an easel pad/whiteboard, ask participants to choose an emotion and, with a partner, describe a time that they have felt the emotion.

Procedure

1. Explain that each person, in turn, will be asked to predict what value the next card in the deck is not. ("The next card is not a _____.") If they are correct, then the game continues.
2. If they do name the card that is flipped over, the round ends.
3. Set a realistic goal for the group (for example, to make it once around the circle) or ask the group to set a goal.
4. Consider playing multiple rounds.
5. Consider allowing participants who are anxious to skip their turn.

Processing

1. Ask participants to write down on a piece of paper three emotions they felt during the activity.
2. Quickly sort the papers and then read the emotions aloud to the group, asking participants to raise their hands if they also felt the shared emotion.
3. Ask for a volunteer with their hand raised to explain what their body felt like (hot, shoulders tight, tired, etc.) when they felt the emotion.
4. What was the consequence if you got the card right? Did your emotion feel stronger than the consequence?

5. How can having a growth mind-set help you with this activity? What about in other areas of your life?

Connections to Content

Language Arts: Participants write a paragraph response to a prompt and then revise with peers at least three times. Compare the original and the final revision to highlight the benefit of a growth mind-set during the revision process.

Mathematics: Provide a pre-assessment of five to ten questions before beginning new content. Mark the assessment based on the effort rather than the accuracy. Ask participants to think about how knowing what you don't know can help you do better.

Social Studies: Read about a historical figure who wasn't recognized for their achievements until after they died (Vincent van Gogh, Gregor Mendel, Emily Dickinson, etc.).

Science: Discuss the connection between a growth mind-set and scientific inquiry.

Facilitation Tip: This activity can be reframed as a consensus-building activity by asking the group to agree on what the next card is not. For a greater challenge, ask participants whether the next card is higher or lower.

Is This Seat Taken?

SEL Competency: Self-Awareness

Objectives

- Participants will recognize emotions and how they affect behavior.
- Participants will be introduced to a growth mind-set.

Materials: A circle of chairs or spot markers

Time: 20 minutes

Warm-Up: Challenge participants to complete two or three age-appropriate brainteaser questions. For instance:

- What are the next three letters in the following sequence? J, F, M, A, M, J, J, A, ___. (Hint: Use a calendar. Answer: S, O, N)
- What is full of holes but can still hold water? (Answer: A sponge)

Procedure

1. Each participant has a place in the circle. The facilitator stands in the middle of the circle to begin the first round.

2. In Level 1, the facilitator explains that the person in the middle will ask the people in chairs if their seat is taken. They will respond with "Yes."

3. While the person in the middle is walking around and asking for a seat, the people in the circle can make eye contact with each other and swap chairs. This provides the person in the middle a chance to take one of the open chairs.

4. In Level 2, participants can simply move whenever they see a chair available, without having to lock eyes.

Processing

1. Raise your hand if you swapped seats. Raise your hand if you never moved. Raise your hand if you got "stuck" in the middle.

2. Ask anyone who raises their hand to explain the reason behind their choice. What emotions did they feel?

3. Ask about risk and growth. Can you grow if you don't take a risk? Who had fun? Everyone? Anyone?

4. Did the people who did not move still participate in some way? Why or why not? What observations did they make?

5. How does working on a brainteaser at the beginning relate to participating in this activity?

 Connections to Content: Ask participants to write a 1-minute reflection about their experience during the activity and how it relates to their academic learning.

Knots

SEL Competency: Self-Awareness

Objectives

- Participants will practice a growth mind-set.
- Participants will practice noticing their emotions.

Materials: None

Time: 10–15 minutes

Warm-Up: Brainstorm times when you have felt stuck. Consider, for example, a time in class working on a tough problem or in a game when you were losing.

Procedure

1. Ask participants to face each other while standing in a tight circle.
2. Each person holds out their right hand and grasps the right hand of someone else, as if they were shaking hands.
3. Then each person extends their left hand and grasps the hand of another person, so that each person is holding the hands of two different people.
4. This hand-in-hand configuration should come out equal.
5. When the participants' hands are tightly held, arms intertwined, and bodies juxtaposed, it is time to explain the problem. The group is to try to unwind themselves from their tangled situation to form a hand-in-hand circle.
6. The physical hand-to-hand contact cannot be broken in order to facilitate the unwinding process. Palms may pivot on one another but contact may not be lost.
7. As a result of the initial connections, and depending on the number of participants, two or even three distinct people circles may form. These circles may be intertwined or people in the final circle(s) may alternate facing directions—that's okay.

Processing

1. What emotions did you notice during the activity?
2. How did you manage your emotions?
3. Have you ever felt a similar way at school?
4. What strategies do you use to manage yourself when you are frustrated?

Connections to Content: Connect the process of untying the knot to understanding your content area. Acknowledge that sometimes failing to ask for help in class can lead to a cascade of challenges that feel insurmountable.

Facilitation Tip: If hand holding is a barrier to this activity, you can ask participants to hold pieces of rope or another object to connect instead of directly hand to hand. This modification may create real knots and be even more challenging.

Gimme That

SEL Competency: Self-Awareness

Objectives

- Participants will identify emotional states that contribute to or detract from their ability to solve problems.
- Participants will describe an experience, including the physical sensations and emotions that accompany it.

Materials: Dice, paper or index cards, pens/pencils, Feelings Cards (p. 198), and an easel pad/whiteboard

Time: 30 minutes

Warm-Up: Play a quick round of Mirror Mirror. Have participants form pairs. Facing each other, they copy the movements and emotion of their partners. When you say "Mirror, mirror," they swap partners.

Procedure

1. Form small groups (three to five people per group).
2. Give each participant a piece of paper or an index card.
3. Give each group one pen/pencil and one die.
4. Explain that each person is trying to number their paper 1–100.
5. In order to get the pen/pencil, they must roll a 5 (or any value you want).
6. They should pass the die around in a circle, taking turns.
7. If someone else rolls a 5, they get the pen/pencil and pass the die on.
8. Continue until all participants have written to 100.

Processing

1. Spread out Feelings Cards and ask participants to make a pile of the emotions that they experienced during the activity. Create a word bank on the easel pad/whiteboard.
2. Ask participants to draw a timeline from the beginning of the block when they played Mirror, Mirror through the reflection time. Label points at which they were experiencing different emotions.
3. Ask participants to reflect on the body sensations they felt during the activities and add them to the timeline.
4. Create a concept map showing emotions and connecting sensations.
5. How did sensations and/or emotions affect behavior during the activity?
6. What are other situations where sensations or emotions can affect behavior or performance?
7. What are some strategies to prevent escalation of negative emotions or behaviors?

 Connections to Content: Discuss content-specific strategies for approaching challenging tasks.

Simply Paper

SEL Competency: Self-Awareness

Objectives

- Participants will demonstrate awareness of how personal experience shapes perspective.
- Participants will explore the difference between a fixed mind-set and a growth mind-set.

Materials: Paper (one piece per participant)

Time: 20 minutes

Warm-Up: Have each participant stand on one foot. Ask how many are standing on their left foot and how many are standing on their right foot. Ask participants to cross their arms on their chests. Ask how many have their left arm closest to their chest, and how many have their right arm. Repeat with folding hands together or touching their nose with a fingertip. Then ask about any patterns they might be noticing. Everyone is hearing the same instructions—why aren't they doing the exact same things?

Procedure

1. Give each participant a sheet of paper.

2. Ask them to close their eyes (or face away from the other members of the group), and then explain that you are going to give them instructions.

3. During the duration of the instructions, they should focus on themselves and wait to ask any questions until the end of the activity.

4. Even if they do have questions, they should continue to follow the instructions to the best of their ability.

5. Read the following instructions aloud:

    a. Take your paper and fold it in half.

    b. Tear off the bottom right-hand corner.

    c. Fold the paper in half again.

    d. Tear off the upper left-hand corner.

    e. Fold the paper in half one more time.

    f. Make a tear in the bottom of the paper in the center.

6. Have the participants open their eyes and turn back to the group. Ask them to unfold their papers and look around the room for anyone who has a paper that is similar to theirs.

Processing

1. Find a partner who has a paper similar to yours. With your partner, share some questions that you wanted to ask during the activity. Explain how you managed when you couldn't ask any questions.

2. Find a new partner with a paper that is very different from yours. Discuss why many papers are different when everyone received the same instructions.

3. When is it helpful to have multiple perspectives? When is it challenging to have multiple perspectives?

4. Explain that when you have a growth mind-set, you believe you are capable of growing and learning from mistakes. When you have a fixed mind-set, you think mistakes define you instead of seeing them as a learning opportunity. When you were following the directions, did you have more of a fixed mind-set or a growth mind-set?

5. How does an activity like this help you practice having a growth mind-set?

6. How else can you practice having a growth mind-set?

 Connections to Content

Language Arts: Start to create a word wall to capture new social-emotional vocabulary and concepts.

Mathematics: Provide participants with a multiple-step problem that has been solved but has at least one error in the process. Challenge the participants to find the mistake.

Social Studies: Read two primary-source documents that provide different perspectives on the same topic.

Science: Introduce the idea of neuroplasticity.

Facilitation Tip: For another conversation focused on communication, ask participants to record their questions on paper while you give the instructions.

Sound Maps

SEL Competency: Self-Awareness

Objectives

- Participants will reflect on how their own perspective affects their interactions with others.
- Participants will reflect on how their expectations shape their experiences.

Materials: Paper, pens/pencils, and an easel pad/whiteboard

Time: 20 minutes

Warm-Up: Ask participants to write or draw for 2–3 minutes about a time when their experience in a situation was very different from what they had expected.

Procedure

1. Give each participant a new piece of paper and ask them to make an X in the middle of the paper.
2. Walk the group outside and have them sit in an open area approximately 30 feet from each other.
3. Ask participants to remain silent for about 5 minutes and to record the sounds they hear on their paper.
4. The sounds should be drawn on the paper in the approximate area in which they are heard (for example, a participant draws a bird or music notes in the bottom left-hand corner of the card if they heard a bird chirping behind them to the left).
5. Encourage participants to be creative and not to worry about their artistic ability.
6. After 5 minutes, ask the group to pair up and use their drawings to discuss with their partner what they heard.

Processing

1. Ask students about the things that they drew and create a master list on an easel pad/whiteboard:
   a. With a show of fingers, how many different things did you draw on your sound map?

b. What did you do when you couldn't draw what you heard?

c. Are there any sounds you heard that aren't on the list? If so, add them to the list in a different color.

d. Was there anything you heard that you weren't expecting? Is there anything that others heard that surprised you?

2. Go back to the reflection from the warm-up: With a partner, share an experience that wasn't the same as you expected, if there was one. What is a commonality you notice about the experiences?

3. Where you sat gave you a certain perspective for the sound map. Similarly, how do your life experiences shape your perspective?

 Connections to Content: Ask participants to think about how their placement in the classroom or in their social groups affects their perspective and experiences at school.

Play a Card

SEL Competency: Self-Awareness

Objectives

- Participants will identify their own strengths and challenges.
- Participants will learn about their peers' strengths and challenges.

Materials: A deck of playing cards

Time: 30 minutes

Warm-Up: Share this Michael Jordan quote: "My attitude is that if you push me towards something that you think is a weakness, then I will turn that perceived weakness into a strength."

Procedure

1. Give each participant a playing card.

2. Explain that the suit of the playing card determines what they share with the group.

    a. Hearts: Something they are passionate about

    b. Diamonds: A personal strength

    c. Clubs: An affinity group they belong to (sports team, church group, extracurricular activity, etc.)

    d. Spades: A personal challenge (something they need to dig into to be successful)

3. Allow participants to swap cards. If they do not have the suit with the question they want to address, they may trade with another participant or draw again from the deck.

4. After all participants have a card they are satisfied with, provide an opportunity to share.

Processing

1. Have participants create small groups based on the suit they chose. Which group is the largest? Smallest? Why?

2. Which suit was the most challenging to answer? Why?

3. As a group, what are we passionate about?

4. What personal strengths exist in this group? What challenges?

5. How are our strengths, challenges, and passions connected to the other groups we belong to?

6. Form pairs in which one person is challenged by something that the other identifies as a strength and discuss the Michael Jordan quote. Do you agree or disagree?

 Connections to Content: Use the format of Play a Card to preview or review academic material. For instance, hearts are what you loved about the reading, diamonds are a key point, clubs are patterns or themes, and spades are hidden gems or key phrases.

Autobiographical Poem

SEL Competency: Self-Awareness

Objectives

- Participants will practice identifying positive characteristics about themselves.
- Participants will articulate personal goals.

Materials: Pens/pencils and copies of the Autobiographical Poem template (p. 194)

Time: 20 minutes

Warm-Up: Have participants choose an animal that represents one of their strengths and share with a partner.

Procedure: Ask participants to write a poem about themselves using the Autobiographical Poem template.

Processing

1. What was challenging about creating this poem?
2. What, if anything, would have been different if you had written this last week? Last month? Last year?

 Connections to Content: Create a biographical poem to describe an important contributor to any specific academic area.

Facilitation Tip: Use photos of animals for the warm-up instead of just asking participants to choose from a list or their memory. By providing a visual prompt, you encourage deeper thinking and learning.

Personal Coat of Arms

SEL Competency: Self-Awareness

Objectives

- Participants will recognize their own strengths and goals.
- Participants will demonstrate awareness of personal and collective identity encompassing strengths, areas for growth, aspirations and cultural assets.

Materials: Image cards or photographs for warm-up, Coat of Arms hand-outs (p. 196), pens/pencils, and an easel pad/whiteboard

Time: 30 minutes

Warm-Up: *For younger participants, consider introducing the concept of metaphors before this activity.* Using image cards or photographs, ask participants to choose one that illustrates a personal strength. Alternatively, share a few examples of coats of arms and brainstorm what the words and symbols might mean.

Procedure

1. Give each participant a copy of the Coat of Arms handout and a pen/pencil.

2. Write six questions on the easel pad/whiteboard, then ask participants to answer each question in the appropriate box by drawing a picture, design, or symbol. Sample questions include:

　a. Who is someone in your life that you look up to?

　b. What is an accomplishment that you are proud of?

　c. What is one thing that you are good at?

　d. What is one goal you have for the next month?

　e. What is one thing you would like to improve about yourself?

　f. What is one goal you hope to accomplish in the next 10 years?

Processing

1. In pairs, explain your shields to each other.

2. In pairs, discuss which question was the most challenging. Which was the easiest question? Why?

3. In combat, shields can be used for protection. How could your shield protect you?

Connections to Content

Language Arts: Write a personal narrative that illustrates the six characteristics you included in your shield and how they can "protect" you. For older participants, explain the concept of protective factors and risk factors.

Mathematics: Discuss budgeting and personal finance.

Social Studies: Explore the crests and flags of countries and states.

Science: Explore natural selection and adaptation of organisms.

Cooperative Tarp

SEL Competency: Self-Awareness

Objectives

- Participants will examine possible outcomes associated with different ways of communicating emotions and feelings.
- Participants will recognize and name their own and other people's emotions.
- Participants will practice flexible and constructive thinking.

Materials: One 4 x 6 foot tarp or heavy blanket

Time: 30 minutes

Warm-Up: Introduce the ABCDE (Ask, Brainstorm, Choose, Do, and Evaluate) model of problem solving. If your school or organization uses a different problem-solving model, you may want to use it instead.

Procedure

1. Lay the tarp or blanket out flat. Ask all participants in the group to stand on it with both feet.
2. The goal is for the group to flip the tarp over without stepping off it or touching the ground around it.
3. The problem has been solved when the entire group is standing on the other side of the tarp.

Processing

1. Did the group have a plan before they started? Did everyone know what the plan was? If not, what prevented some people from knowing the plan?
2. With a show of fingers, how involved were you in the process on a scale of 1 to 4 (4 being the most involved)? Look around. Do you agree with the ratings of your peers? Why or why not?
3. Did your attitude and energy during the activity affect the outcome?
4. What kind of effort did it take for the group to flip the tarp over?
5. How is flipping the tarp similar to changing something in your life that you do not like?

Connections to Content: With a partner, discuss something you find challenging about school or a particular class. Develop a solution-based strategy to address that thing you do not like.

Inside-Out T-Shirts

SEL Competency: Self-Awareness

Objectives

- Participants will recognize their own strengths and goals.
- Participants will demonstrate awareness of personal and collective identity, including strengths, areas for growth, aspirations, and cultural assets.

Materials: T-shirts, copies of the T-shirt template (p. 237), and fabric markers

Time: 30 minutes

Warm-Up: Present this O. Henry quote: "It ain't the roads we take; it's what's inside of us that makes us turn out the way we do." Ask participants to share what the quote means to them.

Procedure

1. Ask participants to design their own T-shirts by putting their positive qualities on the outside of themselves.

2. Participants will design a rough draft on the template, using the prompts below.

3. Encourage participants to focus on themselves. Discourage them from including names of bands, famous athletes, etc., on their shirts.

4. If time permits, participants may decorate the back of the shirts with information about their school or program.

T-Shirt Prompts

- Middle of the shirt: Name
- Under name: Something you are proud of
- Right shoulder: Two things you are good at
- Left shoulder: Something you would like to do or be when you get older
- Top of shirt: Something you value
- Bottom of shirt: Three positive qualities that make you a good friend

Processing

1. What questions were easier to answer?

2. What questions were more difficult to answer?

3. Would we know any of these qualities by just looking at you?

4. Why do we call this activity "Inside-Out"?

 Connections to Content: Focus the questions on any content area.

The "Leader" Ship

SEL Competency: Self-Awareness

Objectives

- Participants will identify characteristics of effective leaders.
- Participants will demonstrate self-awareness.

Materials: Crayons or markers, paper, and an easel pad/whiteboard

Time: 20–30 minutes

Warm-Up: Ask participants to brainstorm qualities a leader should have. Capture this list on an easel pad/whiteboard. After developing a strong list, demonstrate how to draw a particular characteristic. (E.g., if "perceptive" is an attribute of a good leader, draw a ship with many windows so as to see everything that is going on.)

Procedure

1. Explain to the participants that they each will be in charge of an expedition to the planet Pagobe.
2. Their task is to draw a vehicle, equipping it with all the necessary attributes for leading the expedition.
3. They can use the brainstormed list to get started.

Processing

1. What characteristics of a leader did you add to your Leader Ship?
2. Which characteristics do the leaders in your school and community demonstrate?
3. What characteristics of a leader do you have?

 Connections to Content

Language Arts: Read about a youth changemaker and compare their characteristics to the leadership characteristics you illustrated.

Mathematics: What shape represents your leadership style and why?

Social Studies: Name some effective leaders and some ineffective leaders in the world today. What makes them effective or ineffective?

Tap Someone Who

SEL Competency: Self-Awareness

Objectives

- Participants will recognize their own strengths and goals.
- Participants will demonstrate awareness of personal and collective identity, including strengths, areas for growth, aspirations, and cultural assets.

Materials: None

Time: 30 minutes

Warm-Up: Challenge participants to recount the storyline of your time together as a group activity by activity. How did we start? What did we do next? Then what?

Procedure

1. Have the group sit in a circle with their eyes closed.
2. Tap on four participants' shoulders and ask them to stand outside of the circle.
3. At each prompt (five or six each round), the people outside of the circle "tap someone who ..."
4. Make sure everyone gets a chance to be both inside and outside the circle.

Possible Prompts

- makes you laugh
- you wish you knew better
- is a leader
- you admire
- is a friend
- you trust
- you respect
- really lives out loud
- is a good listener
- has helped you
- can brighten your day
- you can depend on
- really carries the team
- you learned from
- has something special to offer
- has made you try harder
- has inspired you
- is fun to be with
- you feel supported by
- you share a secret with
- gives it their all
- is very special to you
- is very strong
- does a good job

- challenges you
- you appreciate
- has done something nice
- has a good sense of humor
- is creative
- has good ideas
- is reliable
- is patient
- is forgiving
- is passionate
- represents the group well
- has dreams
- has values you admire
- you believe in
- shows compassion
- has taught you something
- has given you good advice
- has the ability to make their dreams come true

Processing: Write a note of appreciation to someone in your life who has done one of the above things and pass along the kindness to someone else.

How Did We Do Bingo

SEL Competency: Self-Awareness

Objectives

- Participants will assess themselves on a variety of behaviors.
- Participants will reflect on their emotions, participation, and behavior throughout the day.

Materials: Bingo cards (p. 195) and pens/pencils

Time: 20 minutes

Warm-Up: During your time with the group, pick up mementos and put them in a bag. At the end of the day, unpack the mementos to review the day.

Procedure

Distribute the Bingo cards and instruct the participants: "In looking over how you may have done today, look for five blocks in a row (across or down) that you could answer 'Yes' to. Put a check in those blocks and be prepared to share."

Processing

1. Which action on the card is the easiest to complete? Why?

2. Which action on the card is the hardest to complete? Why?

3. What part of the day was the most challenging for you? Why?

4. What tools did you learn today that you can apply tomorrow?

 Connections to Content: Use a Bingo card to review or preview content. Fill each box with a question and challenge participants to work with a partner to correctly answer questions until they have a BINGO.

Letter to Self

SEL Competency: Self-Awareness

Objectives

- Participants will demonstrate the ability to reflect on effective strategies for managing emotions, thoughts, impulses, and stress.
- Participants will demonstrate self-awareness and understanding external influences.

Materials: Paper, envelopes, and pens/pencils

Time: 30 minutes

Warm-Up: Brainstorm what you would put in a time capsule.

Procedure

1. Give participants paper, an envelope, and a pen/pencil.

2. Explain that they will be writing a letter to themselves about their experiences and their goals.

3. The letter will be held and returned later in the year.

4. Explain that the letter is for them and will not be read by anyone else.

5. Encourage them to do their best work, and remind them that they are worth the effort.

6. Use the following prompts to guide their reflection:

   a. What are some of your strengths and goals?

   b. How are you influenced by external factors, both positively and negatively?

   c. What do you want your future self to remember?

Processing: Invite participants to share some of the things that they wrote in their letter.

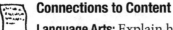 **Connections to Content**

Language Arts: Explain how to address the envelope.

Mathematics: Research the price of postage over time and create a graph.

Social Studies: Write a persuasive letter to a local or state representative about an issue that is important.

Science: Dive into the neuroscience of goal setting and intentions.

Self-Management

One of the first things we did when we got to campus was to carry our bags to the cabins. I had a huge duffle bag that my dad had used in the Reserves, a pillow, and a drawstring bag full of stuff I had brought on the bus for the two-hour ride. I didn't have my cell phone because my teachers had collected it. I met my educator and cabinmates and then searched through the long line of bags to find my stuff.

I was really nervous on the way down to my cabin. I had never stayed away from home before. My dad had told me that I should just try to make it through the first night. I could only face one day at a time. My educator was trying to learn all our names and helped us over the roots and rocks on the trail. I dropped my pillow. The educator helped me brush off the leaves and carried it the rest of the way. When we finally got to the cabin, we were asked to leave our stuff in a pile on the porch and our educator told us we would be settling in later after we had decided on cabin rules.

We then went to the dining hall. I was hungry because I hadn't really had breakfast and was relieved to see there were apples and Goldfish. Our educator told us about "ort," food you take but don't end up eating, and the director told us about the kindness and respect rule. I made a goal to try to be kind and respectful but also know that I sometimes have trouble not being impulsive.

Once we got to class our educator asked us to make goals for the week on a sticky note. I wrote "be kind" although I'm not sure what that really looks like. During our team-building challenge our educator introduced us to SMART goals. They are specific, measurable, achievable, realistic, and timely. I revised my sticky note goal to be kind to at least one new person every day during the week.

At dinner, while we were eating as a cabin group, we ran out of the chicken. I remembered my goal to be kind and offered to get more. On Tuesday, a cabinmate, Sam, needed a pen to write a letter, and I shared mine from my drawstring bag. At the ropes course, I belayed all of my classmates before I took a turn at climbing, not only because I needed to be kind but also because I was really scared about heights.

When I was at Kieve, I needed to do a lot to manage my emotions and behaviors. It was harder than being at home because my family wasn't there to help, but my cabinmates, classmates, and the educators helped me reach my goals. I felt proud on the last day because I had pushed myself to sleep over despite homesickness (and no cell phone), and I had overcome my fear of heights to cross a ropes course element. During the closing activity, our educators reminded us of our growth during the week and the resources available back at school, and encouraged us to keep stretching ourselves.

Being away from home can be a challenging experience, especially if it's the first time. In this vignette, the participant describes their thoughts, feelings, and actions during their week at Kieve Wavus Education. They mention community norms like "Everyone needs to be treated with kindness and respect" and new tools like the "SMART" (Specific, Measurable, Achievable, Realistic, and Timely) goal model. Shared expectations provide clear boundaries and help participants regulate their thoughts, feelings, and behaviors. Setting realistic goals helps maintain motivation. The facilitators provided frequent opportunities to review individual and group goals. At the end of the week, participants reviewed resources in their communities that can support them and help them continue to grow.

Self-management includes regulating emotions, thoughts, and behaviors, as well as effectively managing stress, controlling impulses, and setting and achieving goals. Participants who build self-management skills show immediate and long-term improvement in both mental health and academic achievement.

The first few activities in this section introduce goal setting and personal responsibility. Once the participants have a common understanding of SMART goal setting and group norms, the activities become more physically and emotionally challenging. The Ice Cube Exercise and In a Hat activities are the most introspective activities, while Peanut Butter and Jelly Sandwich, Key Punch, Pipeline, and Traffic Jam more clearly draw attention to self-management by revealing how one's actions, feelings, and behaviors impact others. Consider facilitating a goal-setting activity before beginning a unit project to help participants see the value of planning ahead.

Don't Break the Ice

SEL Competency: Self-Management

Objectives

- Participants will be introduced to the SMART goal model.
- Participants will practice goal setting as a member of a group.

Materials: Spot markers or kickboards (enough for one per participant to start) and rope.

Time: 30 minutes

Warm-Up: Use one example to explain or review the SMART goal model.

Procedure

1. Set the markers or kickboards inside a "pond" created by a rope boundary. Explain that the markers are blocks of ice floating on a pond and all members of the group need to stay on the ice. If they step in the water, everyone needs to restart the round.

2. Help the group set a SMART goal for the challenge. (For example, they may choose to be using only *eight* markers at the end of *20* minutes.)

3. Ask everyone to step over the rope and onto a spot of their choice. Once the group has held their positions for a count of 5, ask the group to carefully step off the markers and out of the circle.

4. Nominate a spokesperson for the group. After each successful round, the group can take away at least one marker and move one to another location. Give a limited time for discussion.

5. After the discussion time has expired, the spokesperson must announce the decisions.

6. After the appropriate markers have been moved, the group repeats Steps 3 through 5. With each successive round, nominate a new spokesperson.

7. In order to create space in the pond, participants are allowed to give one other person a piggyback.

8. When the group has reached their goal and/or time expires, move to processing.

Processing

1. What goal did you set?

2. How did you decide on the number of markers? How did you decide on the time?

3. Was the goal achievable? Was it realistic?

4. Were you successful? Why or why not?

5. Why is it helpful to set SMART goals?

 Connections to Content: Provide participants time to set individual content-area goals using the SMART model.

Facilitation Tip: This is a foundational activity to help participants practice using the SMART goal model. If participants are already well versed in SMART goals, you can modify this activity by labeling the markers with specific individual or group goals and requiring consensus to determine the priority, keeping the most important ones.

Don't Sink the Boat

SEL Competency: Self-Management

Objectives

- Participants will work independently.
- Participants will set a SMART goal.

Materials: One 6 x 6 inch sheet of tin foil per participant, a large jar of pennies, and a water basin that will accommodate multiple foil boats at once.

Time: 10–15 minutes

Warm-Up: Review the SMART goal model.

Procedure

1. Explain to participants that they will be working individually and silently.
2. Their challenge is to build a foil boat that will float and hold the most pennies without sinking.
3. Before the participants begin to build, ask them to jot down the number of pennies they hope their boat will hold.
4. Participants may take their boats to the water basin to test them during the building phase.
5. At the end of the allotted time, have a float-off.

Processing

1. Line up by:
   a. The number of pennies they hoped their boat would hold
   b. The number of attempts they tried
   c. The number of pennies their boat held
2. Who enjoyed working alone?
3. Who glanced at someone else's work?
4. What did you notice?
5. What would you do differently next time?

Connections to Content: This activity highlights the power of trying and revising. It can be effective practice before a longer project or unit of work, especially for participants working on developing a growth mind-set.

Facilitation Tip: Working in groups, repeat the activity. Notice if the boats are more successful.

My Life Brainstorm

SEL Competency: Self-Management

Objectives

- Participants will identify interests, talents, and skills.
- Participants will brainstorm future goals.
- Participants will practice effective communication.

Materials: My Life Worksheet (p. 235) and pens/pencils

Time: 20 minutes

Warm-Up: Allow participants about 15 minutes to respond in writing to the following questions and prompts from the My Life Worksheet:

- What do I enjoy doing?
- What are my talents and skills?
- Who do I admire? Why? (Try to name at least three people. They can be people you know personally or people you've heard about through history or the media.)
- What are five things I hope to have accomplished by my 10-year high school reunion?
- In 10 years, I would like my friends to describe me as: (identify at least three qualities)

Procedure

1. Create pairs of participants.

2. Allow one partner 1 minute to share their responses to all the questions.

3. The other partner should then ask any clarifying questions and be prepared to share a summary of five to ten words about their partner's worksheet with the full group.

4. Allow time for the partners to swap roles, then repeat Steps 2 and 3.

Processing

1. What did you learn about your partner?

2. What patterns did you notice?

3. Are there any surprises?

4. Do you have any further clarifying questions?

5. How can sharing our goals help make them a reality?

 Connections to Content: Use a similar model (individual written response, pair conversation and distillation, and large-group summary) for a class discussion on any topic.

Ice Cube Exercise

SEL Competency: Self-Management

Objectives

- Participants will practice managing stress.
- Participants will discuss coping strategies.

Materials: Ice cubes

Time: 30 minutes

Warm-Up: Introduce the Zones of Regulation (see www.zonesofregulation. com) or other method of classifying emotional experiences.

Procedure

1. Ask participants to sit with one palm facing up.
2. Place an ice cube in each participant's open palm.
3. Encourage them not to move it, drop it, or stop the exercise, but rather to turn their awareness to the physical and emotional sensations they experience as they hold the ice cube until it fully melts.
4. Encourage participants to sit quietly and listen while you ask:
   a. How does it feel?
   b. Where do you feel it? Is it painful or just uncomfortable?
   c. What does it feel like? Tingling? Numbness?
   d. Are you in real danger? Is there a risk of significant injury?
   e. What coping skills are you using to move through the pain you are feeling?
   f. What helps? What makes it worse?
   g. How long do you predict the pain will last after the ice cube melts?

Processing

1. Sometimes when we experience something difficult, we worry that our suffering may never end or that we won't be able to tolerate it. These worries can make the actual experience even harder. Who was worried during this activity?
2. Did you feel other emotions or sensations?
3. What coping skills did you use?

4. Did you think that the pain would eventually go away? If yes, was this helpful?

5. How could this exercise help you the next time you are experiencing discomfort?

 Connections to Content

Language Arts: Write a narrative of the experience, including emotions and senses. Write an alternative ending.

Mathematics: Calculate the amount of time (in minutes, hours, percentages, etc.) you spend doing unpleasant daily tasks during the course of a day.

Social Studies: Explore cultural perspectives of adversity.

Science: How do we feel pain physiologically?

Blind Tree Find

SEL Competency: Self-Management

Objectives

- Participants will practice regulating emotions, thoughts, and behaviors.
- Participants will consider personal and environmental responsibilities.

Materials: Blindfolds or bandannas

Time: 30 minutes

Warm-Up: Bring participants to a large open area. Challenge them to close their eyes and try to locate you using only their sense of hearing while you tap out a beat with two sticks or on a small drum.

Procedure

1. Bring the group to a wooded area.

2. Separate participants into pairs. One participant will be blindfolded and will be the tree detective. Their partner will be the guide.

3. Explain that, when blindfolded, the tree detective must be holding on to either a tree or someone else's hand or shoulder.

4. The guide leads the tree detective through the area and brings them to a specific tree.

5. The tree detective uses touch, smell, and hearing to try to memorize the tree's size, location, and texture.

6. The guide leads the tree detective back to the starting point and takes off the blindfold.

7. The detective tries to locate their tree.

8. Participants then swap roles. Allow time for participants to have at least two rounds in each role.

Processing

1. When you were the detective, how did it feel to be unable to see?

2. When you were the guide, how did it feel to lead someone who was unable to see?

3. What did you do differently when you were the detective? The guide?

4. Do you think you guided differently after you had been a detective?

5. In your daily life, when do you need to use similar skills?

 Connections to Content

Language Arts: Answer a prompt and then pass your response to a peer to be revised and submitted.

Mathematics: Take a short assessment together with a partner.

Social Studies: Discuss the role of elected officials and the responsibility of voters.

Science: Dig into the observations and sensations of the experience, then use identification guides to classify the flora.

Facilitation Tip: If participants aren't comfortable being blindfolded, facilitate the activity with "honesty blindfolds"—also known as just closing their eyes.

In a Hat

SEL Competency: Self-Management

Objectives

- Participants will reflect on common goals and fears.
- Participants will brainstorm what steps can be taken to achieve goals and find resources that can alleviate those fears.

Materials: Paper, pens/pencils, and a hat or bowl

Time: 30 minutes

Warm-Up: Share this Henry Ford quote: "Obstacles are those frightful things you see when you take your eyes off your goal." Explain that the purpose of this activity is to explore both the goals we share and the obstacles we see in our way.

Procedure

1. Give each participant a piece of paper and instruct them to anonymously write either a goal that they have or a worry or concern about the current or upcoming year. Encourage participants to take advantage of the anonymity to write goals or concerns that people might not expect of them. Fold the papers with goals and concerns and place them in the hat or bowl.

2. Read each contribution aloud, either by reading them all yourself or by handing one random goal or concern to each person to read around the circle.

Processing

1. Challenge participants to sort the goals and concerns into categories to uncover themes.

2. In small groups, ask participants to write SMART goals based on the group's theme.

3. Share the theme and SMART goals back to the large group.

 Connections to Content: Repeat a similar process to brainstorm what participants know about a particular topic either as a preview or a review.

Warp Speed

SEL Competency: Self-Management

Objectives

- Participants will practice problem solving and decision making.
- Participants will practice effective communication.
- Participants will recognize cause-and-effect relationships.

Materials: A tennis ball or other tossable object

Time: 30 minutes

Warm-Up: Invite the group to choose the tossable object for the activity.

Procedure

1. Ask everyone to sit or stand in a circle.

2. Explain that the object begins with the facilitator. It must travel to everyone in the circle once, but it may not be passed to a participant's immediate right or left. The last person to receive the object must pass it back to the facilitator.

3. Once they make a passing pattern, ask the group to set a speed goal for themselves. Encourage them to brainstorm different ways to achieve that goal.

4. Allow multiple attempts to reach the goal.

Processing

1. How was the communication during the activity? Which components of effective communication did you notice?

2. What strategies did you try to achieve your goal?

3. If you had known the goal when you began the activity, would you have approached the challenge differently?

4. How can you use what you learned during this activity in other areas of your life?

 Connections to Content

Language Arts: Initiate a conversation about word choice. How can your writing be improved when you improve your vocabulary?

Mathematics: Explore problem-solving strategies.

Social Studies: Create an action plan to address a community issue.

Science: How do patterns in nature help us understand the world around us?

Robot

SEL Competency: Self-Management

Objectives

- Participants will demonstrate personal responsibility to others.
- Participants will evaluate the cause and effect of impulsive behavior.

Materials: None

Time: 30 minutes

Warm-Up: Play a quick round of Delayed Follow the Leader (p. 6). The leader demonstrates an action. When the leader switches to a different action, the group repeats the first one. Continue playing for about a dozen total actions.

Procedure

1. Form pairs.
2. Explain that at any given time, one partner will be a robot and one will be the human in charge of the robot.
3. The human can control the robot by tapping on the robot to indicate instructions.
4. Tap on the robot's head to turn the robot off and on.
5. Tap on the robot's shoulder to turn the robot left and right.
6. Have each human take their robot on a walk to explore the surrounding area and interact with other robots. Then, after a few minutes, have each pair swap roles.
7. After both partners have done both roles, have them try it again with the robot blindfolded.

Processing

1. How did it go?
2. What were the responsibilities of the robots? Of the humans?
3. Those of you who were humans first, how did it change your behavior as a robot?
4. Those of you who were robots first, how did it change your behavior as a human?

5. What strategies did you use to stay focused and safe during this activity?

6. How does knowing our responsibilities or expectations help us reach our goals?

 Connections to Content: After completing this activity, ask participants to work in pairs to complete a task that requires them to have different roles and use effective communication.

Facilitation Tip: For more advanced groups, give more than one robot to each human.

Moon Ball

SEL Competency: Self-Management

Objectives

- Participants will practice goal setting.
- Participants will practice managing stress and maintaining confidence.

Materials: A beach ball or other large lightweight ball

Time: 30 minutes

Warm-Up: Review the SMART goal model.

Procedure

1. Explain that the objective is to see how many times the group can hit the ball in the air without letting it hit the ground.

2. The same person cannot hit the ball twice in a row. If the same person hits the ball twice in a row, it only counts as one hit.

3. Ask the group to set a SMART goal and then proceed with the activity.

4. Depending on time and the determination of the group, increase the challenge by adding more specific rules or changing the group's goal.

Processing

1. Did the group have a clear plan for keeping the ball in the air?

2. Was everyone involved? Was it possible to be involved in the activity and not touch the ball?

3. What emotions did you feel during the activity? How did emotions affect your ability to reach your goal? How did it feel when you reached your goal?

4. Did you use any strategies to stay focused or engaged during the activity? Can you use those strategies to stay engaged at school?

 Connections to Content: This activity has the potential to be very challenging for a group. It may be necessary to thoroughly process different perspectives and personalities before moving on to engage in academic group work.

Facilitation Tip: When a group begins to break down during an activity, making a STOP call and stepping away from the game space can lead to success. STOP is an acronym for pausing in the middle of the chaos and checking in. It stands for Stop, Think, Organize, and Proceed. Anytime a group is struggling with a task, any group member (or you as the facilitator) can make a STOP call. **Stop** the activity and step away from the immediate space. **Think** about what is working (or not working). **Organize** an updated plan. **Proceed** by returning to the task. In a timed activity, the time used to reevaluate counts on the clock can be worth every second.

Peanut Butter and Jelly Sandwich

SEL Competency: Self-Management

Objectives

- Participants will practice articulating a step-by-step process to meet a goal.
- Participants will be introduced to *intent* versus *impact*.

Materials: Bread, peanut butter or sunbutter, jelly, spoons, knives, paper, and pens/pencils

Time: 45 minutes

Warm-Up: Wear shoes with laces. Ask a participant to describe how to tie your shoe. Slowly attempt to follow the instructions. When you misunderstand, introduce the idea of *intent* versus *impact*. (That is, they intended their instruction to cause you to do X, but you interpreted it differently and did Y.)

Procedure

1. Ask each participant to write out step-by-step directions for making a peanut butter and jelly sandwich.

2. Emphasize that participants should not assume anything when writing the directions. They are to imagine that the person who will be making the sandwich has never done it before.

3. After everyone is done, ask for two volunteers. One person will read their directions and the other person will do exactly as the directions say, asking no questions.

4. Repeat with two new volunteers as many times as you can stand it.

Processing

1. What were the consequences of unclear directions?

2. What were the consequences of not being able to ask questions?

3. Why is it important to be clear as well as to ask questions?

Facilitation Tip: Offer to be the volunteer who is following the instructions instead of having a participant follow the instructions. This can help keep the processing responses more consistent and connected to the activity's objectives.

Key Punch

SEL Competency: Self-Management

Objectives

- Participants will practice planning.
- Participants will practice effective communication.
- Participants will consider the cause and effect of impulsive behavior.

Materials: Boundary rope, spot markers or paper plates labeled with letters/numbers, and a stopwatch

Time: 30 minutes

Warm-Up: If using in an academic content area, brainstorm content with participants. If using as a general activity, brainstorm times when participants need to have a plan.

Procedure

1. Divide participants into two smaller groups. The first group will start on one side of the boundary rope. About 30 feet away from the rope is a circle filled with all of the spot markers spread out in random formation.

2. Participants must touch the spots in numeric or alphabetical sequence. Any part of the body may be used to touch a spot. Everyone in the group must be involved.

3. This is a timed activity. Each small group will establish their time on the first attempt. Both small-group times will be added together for an overall total. The group will then try to beat their initial time by planning. The focus can be on all participants collaborating to improve, or you can encourage competition between the small groups. All planning must be done behind the start line.

4. The stopwatch starts when the first person crosses the line and stops when the last person crosses the line.

5. Penalty points are added if two or more people are inside the rope at the same time or if a spot is touched out of sequence (*penalty of 5 seconds added to the time*).

Processing

1. Did the group have a plan? Did everyone know what the plan was?

2. Was it difficult to agree on a plan?

3. How did your actions contribute to the success of your group?

4. Did you use your observations of the other small group to help your own small group be more successful?

 Connections to Content

Label the spots with content-specific information for review/ preview.

Language Arts: Spell words or sequence parts of a story by touching spots.

Mathematics: Write math problems on the spots instead of simple numbers so the problems must be solved before choosing the lowest value.

Social Studies: Review the sequence of important events or the lives of historical figures.

Human Mastermind

SEL Competency: Self-Management

Objectives

- Participants will work collaboratively to complete a challenge.
- Participants will practice clear and effective communication.

Materials: Five spot markers or pieces of felt of different colors

Time: 30 minutes

Warm-Up: Present a few brainteasers:

1. Imagine that there are three playing cards in a row. There is a two to the right of a king. There is a diamond to the left of a spade. There is an ace to the left of a heart. There is a heart to the left of a spade. Identify the three cards. (Answer: An ace of diamonds, a king of hearts, and a two of spades)

2. Give participants seven letter tiles (N, W, O, E, O, R, D) and challenge them to spell one word using all of the tiles. (Answer: ONE WORD)

3. What four-letter word can be written forward, backward, or upside down and still be read from left to right? (Answer: NOON)

Procedure

1. Place the five spot markers or pieces of felt on the floor in a straight line, then privately draw a grid representing the five markers and place a group member's name on each spot.

2. The group's goal is to figure out what names the facilitator wrote down and the order of those names.

3. Challenge the group to set a goal of how many turns it will take to solve the problem.

4. One participant moves to each marker.

5. When participants have filled each marker, the facilitator will let the group know how many people are correct and how many of those people are on the correct spots.

6. The group repeats Steps 4 and 5 until the problem is solved or they run out of turns.

Processing

1. Did you make a plan? Did you follow it?

2. Was there a leader?

3. What was difficult about the challenge?

4. Did anyone get frustrated? Why? How did you deal with frustration?

5. What would you do differently if you had an opportunity to do the challenge again?

 Connections to Content: When participants are struggling with a particular skill or expectation, completing this challenge can help them recognize that having a consistent and organized plan is important for making positive change.

Traffic Jam

SEL Competency: Self-Management

Objectives

- Participants will describe common and creative strategies for overcoming or mitigating obstacles.
- Participants will practice clear and effective communication.
- Participants will reflect on how personal choices affect group success.

Materials: Objects to stand on, pennies to practice, and chenille stems to reflect

Time: 30 minutes

Warm-Up: Ask participants to jot down two or three personal goals and the obstacles they might encounter along the way.

Procedure

1. Divide group in half. If there are ten members, five stand or sit on objects (paper plates, taped-out areas, spot markers, chairs, etc.) facing the other five on similar objects, with one empty object between them. (Therefore, eleven objects in all.) The goal is for the groups to exchange places.

2. Objects may be arranged in a semicircle so that everyone can see the action.

3. Explain these rules to the participants:

    a. You may only move forward.

    b. No one can step back.

    c. You may only move to an empty space.

    d. You may only pass someone facing the opposite way you are.

    e. You may only pass one person at a time.

    f. You must remain facing the same way that you started.

    g. If there's a traffic jam, you must start again.

Processing

1. What were some obstacles you encountered during the activity?

2. When you hit a traffic jam in real life, you can't just start over. What are some strategies that you use when you encounter obstacles en route to your goal?

3. Transform a chenille stem into a representation of a path to a current personal goal. Share your representation with the group.

4. How can you all work collectively to help each other meet individual goals?

Facilitation Tip: Practice this activity with lines of pennies to identify successful patterns.

Pipeline

SEL Competency: Self-Management

Objectives

- Participants will practice using the STOP acronym.
- Participants will practice working as a team.
- Participants will practice clear and effective communication.

Materials: One piece of PVC pipe for each participant (½ inch diameter by 12 inches long, cut in half lengthwise), two marbles, two buckets or cans in which to collect marbles, and a processing tool such as Feelings Cards (p. 198).

Time: 30 minutes

Warm-Up: Introduce or review the STOP acronym (p. 65). Ask participants to brainstorm times that STOP would be helpful.

Procedure

1. Divide the group into two teams. Place each team's bucket or can against the wall. The bucket cannot be moved.

2. Give one piece of PVC pipe to each participant.

3. Level 1: Each team rolls a marble freely through everyone's pipe and into the can. If it touches anyone's thumbs or fingers or falls out of a pipe, start over.

4. Level 2: Do it again with the same rules as above, plus the pipes cannot touch.

5. Bring the teams back into a circle and discuss their successes and failures.

6. Most groups will solve these two levels by making a long ramp of their pipes and dropping the marble from one person to the next. Explain that since this solution doesn't allow for any *control* of the marble, the group will need to try another method.

7. Review the STOP acronym.

8. Level 3: Tell the group that when each person gets the marble, it is their responsibility to *stop* the marble, *think* about how they will get *organized* with the person next to them, and then *proceed* to pass the marble on. The new goal is to pass the marble all the way around the circle using the rules from Level 2.

9. If the marble drops, start with the person after the one who dropped it. Tell the group they can only make three attempts. The activity is not about making it around the circle, but about the process.

Processing

1. Spread out a processing tool (Feelings Cards, images, body parts, etc.) and ask participants to choose an object or card that illustrates how they felt before the STOP acronym was used. Create a pile of those items.

2. Then ask participants to choose an object or card that illustrates how they felt in Level 3, *after* they were given the STOP tool. Create a different pile.

3. How do tools like the STOP acronym help you succeed at reaching your goals?

4. What are some other strategies you used to be successful in this activity?

 Connections to Content

Mathematics: Teach a scaffolded method to solve logic or word problems.

Social Studies: Explore how the democratic process ideally works to create positive change.

Science: Explore the scientific process. Read about researchers learning new and interesting things.

Relationship Skills

When our classroom educator showed us the map in the morning, everyone's eyes gravitated toward the Blind Maze. I, for one, felt nervous. Rumors flew around as we walked from activity to activity and, during snack, I saw what I thought was a blindfold poking out from the top of our educator's backpack.

After snack, we made a magnetic circle. (It took us a while and our classroom educator could have gotten frustrated with us, but they stayed calm and patient until we eventually got it.) The maze, said the educator, was somewhere on the Kieve campus. They wouldn't tell us where the maze was, or how big it was. The only thing they told us was that we could raise our hands and ask one of two questions, "Can I have some help?" or "Have I found the solution?" After we put on our blindfolds, I had a hunch that someone would be peeking. (He always peeks when his eyes are supposed to closed.) Naturally, this meant I decided to lift up my own blindfold and sneak a peek. I was right, he was peeking.

Eventually, we formed a blindfolded conga line with our non-blindfolded educator at the front. When our line reached wherever the maze was (it took us a while—Darius's fault!), we stopped. Everything fell silent, and our educator began to lead us one by one into the maze. Soon, I realized there was a problem—a huge problem. It seemed as if I was trapped in a teeny triangle of rope with no way out.

By this point I had started to think about the two questions we were allowed to ask. ("Have I found the solution?" and "Can I have some help?") But unless the solution was that there was no way out (which isn't much of a solution), I figured that at some point I should ask for help. But that point wasn't now. I don't really like asking for help, so I kept floundering around in this one-square-foot triangle for another five minutes. When I got bored of that, I raised my hand and asked, "Can I have some help?" And then the strangest thing happened—a hand tapped me on the shoulder, and led me out of the maze.

Now I'm not going to say whether I was the first person or the last person to make it out of the maze, but I will say that I made it out before Darius. And I will also say that when Darius did finally raise his hand, I was the one who took his hand and led him out of the Blind Maze.

The activity that the participant describes in this vignette, Blind Maze, is all about help. The facilitator is a guide throughout the experience, modeling calmness and patience before and during the challenge. The participant narrates his feelings as he problem-solves and illustrates his perspective on his peers' behavior and internal conflict about helping. When asking for help, it's easiest to have established relationships. The Blind Maze activity emphasizes individual decision making and asking for help, while other activities in this section focus on building relationships and communication skills.

Relationship skills are about building and sustaining healthy relationships with diverse individuals and groups. Skills include effective communication, conflict resolution, and seeking and offering help. While self-awareness and self-management primarily direct the participants' attention inward, relationship skills require reaching out and building community.

This section builds on the eight guidelines for clear and effective communication, also known as LEADSTAR (p. 5). This section also introduces the new concepts of styles of communication, consensus building, cooperation, and collaboration. The first seven activities allow participants to hone their communication skills before working collaboratively to problem-solve. Many of these activities are easily adapted to be used in content areas to preview or review content.

The Wright Family

SEL Competency: Relationship Skills

Objectives

- Participants will identify behaviors that lead to poor communication.
- Participants will identify how their actions can affect others.

Materials: A soft tossable object for every participant, and the "Life With the Wright Family" story (p. 80) and questions

Time: 20 minutes

Warm-Up: Ask the group to form a circle. Introduce four commands: "Front," "Back," "Right," and "Left." In Level 1, when you give the command, they should jump one step in that direction and repeat the command back to you. When they have mastered Level 1, add confusion by asking them to do the opposite of your command while still repeating the command. For a greater challenge, add a third level during which they follow the direction while saying the opposite.

Procedure

1. Give each participant an object and ask them to form a circle. They can be standing, seated in a chair, or sitting on the ground, but they must all be doing the same thing.
2. Tell the participants that you are going to read them a story and there will be a quiz on the content of the story when you are finished.
3. Tell them that every time you say "Right," they will pass the object in their hands one person to the right, and every time you say "Left," they will pass the object in their hands one person to the left.
4. If an object gets dropped, the participants may pick it up and continue to pass it, but at no time may an object be thrown.
5. Ask if there are any questions to clarify directions.
6. After responding to all questions, begin reading the story. Don't feel the need to speak up and talk over them if they start to get loud, and don't stop reading in a normal, steady voice.
7. When the story is finished, ask them to freeze and set the objects in front of them.

8. Ask a few questions about the story. (Some possible questions are on p. 81.) Ask participants to raise their hand if they know the answer to see how many know it. Select someone to answer.

9. Now that they know what's coming, it can be beneficial to do another round.

Processing

1. Ask someone to repeat the instructions to the group and then ask how it went.

2. Were the questions hard to answer? Why? Is there anything the group could have done to make the challenge easier?

3. Does people being silly, side conversations, interrupting, or other distractions ever happen outside of this activity?

 ### Connections to Content

Language Arts: Ask participants to compose similar stories that involve processing content and moving around.

Facilitation Tip: Depending on your group dynamic and how you'd like to frame the activity, it can be beneficial to let participants hold on to the objects while you begin to debrief. If they identify that distractions made the activity more difficult, you can relate it to real-life examples, like playing with something when they could be participating in a discussion with the group. Using your discretion as the facilitator, you may add extra guidelines to this activity (no talking, only use one hand, stay seated, etc.). Alternatively, you can do the activity without objects, having participants move their own bodies instead.

Life With the Wright Family

One day, the Wright family decided to take a vacation. The first thing they had to decide was who would be left at home, since there was not enough room in the Wright family car for all of them. Mr. Wright decided that Aunt Linda Wright would be the one left at home. Of course, this made Aunt Linda Wright so mad that she left the house immediately, yelling, "It will be a right cold day before I return."

The Wright family now bundled up the children—Tommy Wright, Susan Wright, Timmy Wright, and Shelly Wright—and got in the car and left. Unfortunately, as they turned out of the driveway, someone had left a trash can in the street, so they had to turn right around and stop the car. They told Tommy Wright to get out of the car and move the trash can so they could get going. Tommy took so long that they almost left him in the street. Once the Wright family got on the road, Mother Wright wondered if she had left the stove on. Father Wright told her not to worry: he had checked the stove, and she had not left it on. As they turned right at the corner, everyone started to think about other things that they might have left undone.

No need to worry now, they were off on a right fine vacation. When they arrived at the gas station, Father Wright put gas in the car and then discovered that he had left his wallet at home. So Timmy Wright ran home to get the money that had been left behind. After Timmy had left, Susan Wright started to feel sick. She left the car, saying that she had to throw up. This, of course, got Mother Wright's attention, and she left the car in a hurry. Shelly Wright wanted to watch Susan get sick, so she left the car too. Father Wright was left with Tommy Wright, who was playing a game in the back seat.

With all of this going on, Father Wright decided that this was not the right time to take a vacation, so he gathered up all of the family and left the gas station as quickly as he could. When he arrived home, he turned left into the driveway and said, "I wish the Wright family had never left the house today!"

Possible Quiz Questions

- What is the aunt's first name?
  Linda

- What are the names of the four kids?
  Tommy, Timmy, Shelly, and Susan

- Who was left at home?
  Aunt Linda

- What was left in the street? Who got out to move it?
  Trash can; Tommy

- What was left at home?
  Father Wright's wallet

- What did Mother Wright think she had left on at home?
  The oven

- Where was the Wright family going?
  Vacation

- How far did they get?
  Gas station

- Who got sick?
  Susan

- Who got out of the car to watch?
  Mother Wright and Shelly

- What two people were left in the car?
  Father Wright and Tommy

- What was Tommy doing in the back seat?
  Playing games

Line-Ups

SEL Competency: Relationship Skills

Objectives

- Participants will give examples of nonverbal communication.
- Participants will use nonverbal communication to solve a problem.

Materials: None

Time: 10 minutes

Warm-Up: Invite participants to form a standing circle. Introduce two commands: "Me" (say your own name) and "You" (say the other person's name). Ask a volunteer to stand in the middle of the circle and move around asking "Me?" or "You?" The participant must answer with the correct name. If the participant delays or responds incorrectly, they swap places with the person in the middle.

Procedure

Without speaking, writing, or mouthing words, all the participants must get into a specific order using nonverbal communication. Some line-up suggestions include alphabetically by middle initial, alphabetically by city of birth, or by birthday.

Processing

1. What were some of the messages you were sending during the activity?

2. How did you send messages?

3. How do people send positive messages nonverbally?

4. How do people send negative messages nonverbally?

 Connections to Content

Language Arts: Line up in alphabetical order by name, birth month, favorite animal, etc.

Math: Use dominoes as prompts for the line-up. Participants might line up by total dots or number of top dots, or maybe even look at them as fractions.

Social Studies: Role-play historical figures and create a timeline.

Science: Discuss the observational skills used to figure out the order of the line-up.

Facilitation Tip: This activity is a great litmus test of a group's nonverbal communication skills.

Xerox

SEL Competency: Relationship Skills

Objectives

- Participants will practice effective communication, including active-listening skills.
- Participants will offer and accept constructive feedback.

Materials: Paper, pens/pencils, and copies of designs (p. 239)

Time: 15 minutes

Warm-Up: Form pairs and ask each pair to choose an engineer and a builder. Discreetly tell the engineers that they need to coach their builders to create a paper airplane without using the words *paper* or *airplane*. Allow 5 minutes for the construction and then have a flight test. (See Paper Airplanes, p. 120.)

Procedure

1. One participant is chosen from the group to receive a piece of paper with a design on it. That person must describe the image to the rest of the group so that they can duplicate it.
2. The artist may not show their design to the leader to check its accuracy until the activity is complete.
3. This exercise should be done more than once, with each variation allowing different forms of communication between the leader and the artist. Each version should have a new leader.

Variations

- The leader may only use nonverbal communication to explain the design.
- The leader can say anything but must face away from the group.
- The leader cannot make gestures, and the artists may not ask questions.
- The leader may speak and make gestures, and the artists may ask one question each.
- Leaders and artists can work back to back in pairs with one leader and one artist per group.

Processing

1. How could you tell the artists were listening?

2. What are some qualities or behaviors of an *active* listener? How can listeners be involved in the conversation?

3. What makes it difficult to communicate individually? In a group?

4. How can we improve our communication individually? In a group?

 ### Connections to Content

Use this activity to highlight the benefits of being specific with language and asking questions.

Language Arts: Write a narrative that describes a procedural task or check out the variety in instruction books.

Mathematics: Use geometric shapes as the designs and run as above.

Social Studies: Challenge participants to find a law that doesn't make sense to them and research what it means.

Science: Practice describing a thing without saying what it is (body parts, parts of a flower, etc.).

Facilitation Tip: Use classroom manipulatives instead of pencil and paper to add a kinesthetic twist to the process.

Eyes, Mouth, Body

SEL Competency: Relationship Skills

Objectives

- Participants will practice clear and effective communication.
- Participants will work cooperatively.

Materials: Blindfolds or bandannas (two for every group of three), a random assortment of objects to retrieve (one object for every group of three), and one boundary rope

Time: 30 minutes

Warm-Up: If participants have not completed Robot (p. 62), begin with that activity before moving to this one. If participants are familiar with Robot, play one quick round before diving into this activity.

Procedure

1. Divide the group into teams of three.
2. Explain that each trio works as a team to devise a mode of communication that will help the group to safely retrieve an object that the facilitator will place roughly 30 feet from the boundary line.
3. Each member of the team selects a role. A person can be either EYES, MOUTH, or BODY. Together the group forms a complete person.
4. EYES can see, but can't talk. MOUTH can talk, but can't see. BODY is allowed to talk, can't see, and is the only person who can retrieve the object.
5. *NOTE: The EYES and MOUTH must remain behind the boundary line while the BODY is retrieving the object.
6. Each team has 3–4 minutes to create a plan.
7. When the planning time has expired, the BODIES put on a blindfold. The facilitator then hides one object per group on the ground approximately 30 feet from the boundary line.
8. When the facilitator says "Go," the activity begins and all BODIES enter the area to retrieve their objects. The facilitator and any other support staff act as spotters to reduce the risk of BODIES getting injured.
9. Once the designated object has been retrieved, it must be carried by the BODY (who is still blindfolded) back across the line.

10. Once the last object has been retrieved and carried across the line, ask each team to discuss how well their plan went. Discuss any revisions in their mode of communication, and change roles.

11. In the second and third rounds, the objects may be hidden off the ground but within arm's reach.

Processing

1. What was difficult about the activity?

2. Did your team have an effective mode of communication?

3. Did your team have any breakdowns in communication? If so, how did you deal with these challenges?

4. What did it feel like in the first role you played? How did the last role feel to you?

5. When you were blindfolded, did you feel as though you could trust your teammates? If so, what did the other members of your team do that helped you feel secure and safe?

6. What did you learn from this activity that would be helpful to apply to other teams you play on or participate in?

 Connections to Content: This activity can be used to build trust and to demonstrate various roles in team activities.

Claytionary

SEL Competency: Relationship Skills

Objectives

- Participants will practice clear and effective communication.
- Participants will demonstrate content knowledge.

Materials: One softball-sized ball of clay or playdough for each group of four to five participants

Time: 30–40 minutes

Warm-Up: Brainstorm content-area vocabulary. If you want to reinforce communication skills, the vocabulary could be about effective communication. If you are looking for an active review of a recent reading assignment, consider brainstorming that vocabulary. Then refer to that list during the challenge.

Procedure

1. Separate participants into groups of four or five. Give each group a ball of clay or playdough.
2. Explain that participants are to come to the facilitator, one at a time, from their group to be told what to make.
3. When the facilitator says "Go," the participant tries to make the assigned object for their group. The participant who is building may not talk. The other members of the group try to guess what is being made.
4. Once the object is guessed, the next participant receives a new instruction and Step 3 repeats.

Processing

1. How did listening play a role in this activity?
2. What were some important communication skills you needed to be successful?
3. What was challenging? Why?
4. What did your group do well? Why?
5. What would you do differently if you did this activity again?

 Connections to Content: This activity is very flexible and useful when previewing or reviewing content-area vocabulary.

90

1, 2, 3 = 20 (Turnstile)

SEL Competency: Relationship Skills

Objectives

- Participants will have the opportunity to collaborate to problem-solve.
- Participants will demonstrate team building to reach a goal.
- Participants will practice effective communication.

Materials: One 30 foot rope

Time: 30 minutes

Warm-Up: Wiggle the rope like a snake on the ground and have participants jump over the snake to practice the skill of navigating a large rope.

Procedure

1. Gather participants on one side of the rope. With another staff member, use rope to make a large, revolving jump rope, which is now called the *porthole*. (The loop should be large enough for participants to run through.)
2. Explain to the group that they must pass through the porthole according to the riddle "1, 2, 3 = 20." When they have committed an error, the facilitator will stop the porthole (that is, drop the rope) and give feedback. This new information can be used by the group to help solve the riddle.
3. Each member of the group must pass through the porthole as the staff counts from 1 to 20 during each rotation. Once they have all passed through properly, process the activity.
4. The answer to the riddle: The team must pass through the porthole in the order of one person, two people, three people, one person, two people, three people, etc., for twenty successive porthole rotations. When they deviate from this pattern, drop the rope and give feedback.

Processing

1. What did you think of this activity?
2. How well did the group work together?
3. What was challenging?
4. What would you do differently if you did it again?
5. What would you like to have seen differently from the group?

Two on a Crayon

SEL Competency: Relationship Skills

Objectives

- Participants will communicate without using words.
- Participants will be introduced to three styles of behavior/ communication (passive, assertive, and aggressive).

Materials: Paper and crayons

Time: 20 minutes

Warm-Up: Introduce the terms *passive*, *assertive*, and *aggressive*. If time allows, brainstorm examples and role-play a few.

Procedure

1. Divide participants into pairs and ask them to sit together at a table.
2. Give each pair one crayon and a sheet of paper.
3. Explain that they cannot talk or plan and that they will have to draw a picture as a team without using any words.
4. Both partners hold the crayon at the same time and draw a picture without talking or letting go of the crayon.

Processing

1. Was it difficult not to talk to your partner? Why or why not?
2. Did both members of the pair have an equal role in drawing the picture?
3. Who was the leader? How did you know?
4. How did you communicate with each other during the activity?
5. Was there ever a time you and your partner disagreed? How could you tell?
6. How did you work out any disagreements?

 Connections to Content: Ask participants to respond to a prompt, question, or quiz by drawing.

Squiggle Lines

SEL Competency: Relationship Skills

Objectives

- Participants will practice clear and effective communication.
- Participants will practice cooperation.

Materials: Large drawing paper and crayons or markers

Time: 15–20 minutes

Procedure

1. Divide the participants into groups of four or five. Give each group an identical sheet of large drawing paper with a "squiggle" drawn on it in black marker. At this point, each group's paper is the same as all the others.

2. Each group goes to a separate area of the room so the groups can't overhear each other. Participants brainstorm ideas for what the squiggle might be turned into. Encourage them to look at the paper from each of the four directions. Instruct the participants to agree on what they as a group want to turn their squiggle into.

3. When all the groups have their ideas, distribute one crayon or marker to each participant, giving each participant in a group a different color. The participant may use only the crayon or marker they are given so that each color represents the work of a single participant. Instruct the participants to write their name on the paper using their color.

4. Each group adds to the squiggle to complete the picture they decided on. The group decides what to draw where, and each aspect of the drawing is completed by the participant with the appropriate color crayon or marker. Encourage the groups to add final details and choose a title for their drawing.

Processing

1. Did every member of your group share ideas?

2. Were you surprised when you saw your original squiggle at the end of the activity?

3. Have you ever had an original idea or comment turn out differently because of the influence of others?

Connections to Content

Language Arts: Group members collaborate to write a story by alternating writing sentences from different character perspectives.

Mathematics: Group members collaborate to solve a word problem.

Social Studies: Host a debate or mock trial during which participants work collaboratively to present the argument.

Science: Begin a lab by giving all groups the same materials to explore the same question. Ask participants to design and conduct their specific experiments.

Relationship Skills

95

Scrabble

SEL Competency: Relationship Skills

Objectives
- Participants will collaborate.
- Participants will review components of effective communication.

Materials: Scrabble set made from wooden building blocks (see p. 236), pens/pencils, paper, boundary ropes, and a hula hoop

Time: 30 minutes

Warm-Up: Ask participants to journal for 2–3 minutes about how they communicate. If you are working with younger participants, construct a word list or word wall to scaffold the spelling for the activity. If you are using this activity to review a specific topic, have participants free-write on that topic instead.

Procedure

1. Place the Scrabble blocks inside the hula hoop on the floor in the middle of the room.
2. Divide the group into four even teams. Give each team a piece of paper and a pen/pencil.
3. Place each team in a corner of the room, behind a boundary rope.
4. Explain that groups will be playing a game of Scrabble. The objective is to find words that have a high point value.
5. There will be three rounds. In each round, the teams will be given a category and will have 4 minutes to brainstorm words in that category.
   a. Round 1: Practice round—favorite flavor of ice cream (e.g., chocolate, vanilla, strawberry)
   b. Round 2: When do people need to communicate?
   c. Round 3: How do people communicate?
6. There is a time limit of 3 minutes for each round. During that time, the players from each team take turns running into the middle of the room to bring back one block from the hula hoop.
7. Team members must take turns, and all individuals must be involved. However, one participant can stay behind and be the word builder if the group agrees that they want a person to do that.

8. At the end of the time limit, teams count their scores. If a team has unfinished words or unused letters, those point values are subtracted from their scores. This prevents teams from stockpiling the letters.

Processing

1. What are some strategies of effective communication that you used during the activity?

2. What roles did you have during the activity?

3. Which part of effective communication is the hardest for you? Why?

 Connections to Content: Play Scrabble to preview or review vocabulary, including important people, places, or things.

Blind Maze

SEL Competency: Relationship Skills

Objectives

- Participants will identify family, peer, school, and community resources available to provide support.
- Participants will take ownership of their decisions and recognize when to ask for help and who they can ask.

Materials: Rope connecting trees in a "maze," and blindfolds or bandannas (one for each participant)

Time: 30 minutes

Warm-Up: If participants have not yet completed a blindfold activity, initiate a quick round of Robot (p. 62) or another blindfolded challenge first.

Procedure

1. Explain the instructions: "The next activity is an individual challenge in a maze. You will wear a blindfold into a rope maze and find the solution by yourself by moving along the rope. For safety, please move slowly through the maze, keeping your hands on the rope. Unlike many of our other challenges, this is an individual activity. It is also a silent activity. During the activity, you can raise your hand to ask for help or to ask if you are out of the maze."

2. Take participants close to the maze, but not directly near it.

3. Have them form a single-file line, put their blindfolds on, and walk in a sherpa line (with hands on shoulders) to the blind maze.

4. Guide each participant into the maze and place their hands on the rope.

5. Remind them that they must keep their hands on the rope at all times.

6. Emphasize that there is a way out and that they can always ask for help.

7. Let them travel around the maze, keeping their hands on the rope.

8. When a participant asks for help, gently guide them from the maze and take their blindfold off.

9. Once they are away from the maze, quietly tell them that the way out was to ask for help.

10. Participants who are out of the maze may help other participants exit the maze when they raise their hands and ask for help

11. End the activity when only two or three participants remain in the maze.

Processing

1. What was the purpose of the activity?

2. Why did it take some people a long time?

3. Why is it hard to ask for help?

4. Who in your life do you ask for help?

5. Are there some things you cannot accomplish without help?

6. What are some examples of times in your life when you need help?

 Connections to Content: Ask participants to individually reflect on an area in their life where they need help and brainstorm two or three resources that could help them.

Skittles in a Jar

SEL Competency: Relationship Skills

Objectives

- Participants will practice effective communication.
- Participants will practice consensus building with partners and in larger groups.
- Participants will explore the concept of peer influence on decisions.

Materials: One jar full of Skittles, paper, and pens/pencils

Warm-Up: Ask the group, "What's more important: getting the right answer to a question, or all agreeing on the answer?"

Procedure

1. Distribute one piece of paper and one pen/pencil to each participant.
2. Show each participant the jar of Skittles. Ask them to guess how many Skittles are in the jar without talking to anyone around them. Ask them to write the number down.
3. Ask participants to form pairs and together develop a second guess. Write that guess underneath the first guess.
4. Combine participants into successively larger groups until you either have two groups comprising half of the class each or you have the whole class in one group, documenting a new consensus guess at each interval/ new group along the way.
5. Tell the participants how many Skittles are in the jar and divide them evenly among them.

Processing

1. Which guess did you think was the best guess?
2. Did you move away from that guess, or not?
3. How did your peers influence your decision?
4. Was the peer influence positive or negative?
5. Was getting the right answer or building consensus more important to you?

Connections to Content

Language Arts: Use a similar process to write a creative piece of writing in small groups.

Mathematics: Calculate probabilities or create graphic representations of the data.

Social Studies: Explore different government models and ways of making decisions.

Science: Explore psychology and decision-making strategies.

Relationship Skills

Bull Ring

SEL Competency: Relationship Skills

Objectives

- Participants will use problem-solving skills in a small group.
- Participants will practice using effective communication.

Materials: Some items to use as obstacles, a tennis ball, a can or bucket, and a bull ring (a 2 inch metal or plastic ring with strings attached to it, see p. 181)

Time: 20–30 minutes

Warm-Up: Review LEADSTAR (p. 5) and ask what else we need to think about in order to communicate effectively. What about tone? What does it mean if someone is being passive, assertive, or aggressive?

Procedure

1. Create a large open space with a few obstacles.
2. Lay the bull ring on the ground with the strings spread out like the rays of the sun. Place the tennis ball on the ring.
3. Invite everyone to take their own string and hold it taut at least a foot from the ring.
4. No one can touch the tennis ball or the ring.
5. The tennis ball must be lifted at least 2 inches off the ground before it is moved horizontally.
6. Participants must stay at string's length from the ball.
7. If the ball falls, participants must stop where they are, put the ring back on the ground, and wait for the facilitator to place the ball back onto the ring.
8. The goal is to move the ball to the can or bucket.

Processing

1. What made this activity difficult? How did you compensate?
2. Rate your communication effectiveness from 1 to 10. Why did you choose that number?
3. Who made decisions? Why?
4. Was there just one leader? Identify various leadership roles.
5. How well did your group cooperate? What could you have done better?

Variations

- Use balls of different sizes.
- Work in partner teams with one person blindfolded.
- Work in partner teams in which one partner can only touch the string and the other can only talk.

Cooperation Puzzle

SEL Competency: Relationship Skills

Objectives

- Participants will collaborate to solve a problem.
- Participants will have the opportunity to offer help.

Materials: Cooperation Puzzles in envelopes (see p. 197)

Time: 30 minutes

Warm-Up: Place a pile of rope on the floor and challenge the group to decide, without touching the rope, whether straightening it out will create a knot. Then pull the rope to see whether it does or not.

Procedure

1. Assemble participants in groups of four.
2. Give each group a set of four envelopes. Each group should divide up their envelopes among participants.
3. Have each participant open their envelope, remove the pieces, and spread them on the floor or other flat surface.
4. Without talking or writing, each group must try to assemble the puzzle squares. No player may *take* a puzzle piece from another player; pieces must be *given*.
5. When one group has completed its puzzles, all groups stop.

Processing

1. Were you ever frustrated during the activity?
2. Was it aggravating to see a piece that you needed and have to wait until the person gave it to you?
3. Would talking have helped? Would it have hurt?
4. What did you learn about teamwork?

Helium Stick

SEL Competency: Relationship Skills

Objectives

- Participants will utilize a variety of communication skills while needing to stay calm.
- Participants will develop appropriate problem-solving strategies.
- Participants will practice working as a team.

Materials: One PVC pipe or tent pole, ½ inch (diameter) by 10 feet (length), and an easel pad/whiteboard

Time: 30 minutes

Warm-Up: Write the phrase "That was some trip" on an easel pad/whiteboard. Ask participants to work with a partner to say the phrase at least three different ways. Ask volunteers to demonstrate. Can they sound sarcastic?

Excited? Relieved? Ask participants if they know what "tone of voice" means. Ask for anyone who has ever been told to "watch their tone" to raise their hands. Ask them to pull their ears if they have ever wished someone used a different tone. Ask them to push their nose if they have ever wished they had used a different tone of voice. Explain that sometimes tensions run high during this activity and it will be important to pay attention to their tone of voice.

Procedure

1. Position the group around the pipe/pole.

2. Participants hold their hands out at shoulder height.

3. Each participant should then connect their thumbs and point their index fingers out toward the person across from them.

4. Place the pipe/pole across all fingers where the tips meet.

5. The goal is to lower the pipe/pole to the ground without letting it lose contact with everyone's fingers.

6. If a participant loses contact, the group must begin again from shoulder level.

Processing

1. What were your reactions to the task at hand?

2. How did your reactions affect your actions?

3. How did one person's actions affect the others?

4. What strategies helped you solve the problem?

5. Did this challenge remind you of something you have experienced with others before? If so, what?

 ### Connections to Content

Language Arts: Work more with tone of voice either through speaking or writing.

Mathematics: Provide a challenging problem set and encourage participants to solve it in pairs.

Social Studies: Read two or three primary sources demonstrating different perspectives. Discuss how the tone of the writing contributes to the reader's ability to see the author's perspective.

Science: Explore how other organisms communicate with one another.

Racoon Circles

SEL Competency: Relationship Skills

Objectives

- Participants will demonstrate clear and effective communication.
- Participants will practice problem solving.

Materials: One racoon circle (see p. 182)

Time: 30 minutes

Warm-Up: Challenge the participants to make a square or other shape while all holding the racoon circle. Is everyone contributing equally?

Procedure

1. All participants stand in a circle while holding the racoon circle with both hands.
2. Level 1: Instruct participants to lean back while keeping their legs and backs straight and feet planted, hanging on to the webbing with their hands and relying on it to support them from falling all the way back.
3. Level 2: Instruct participants to go down to a seated position while keeping their weight on the webbing and then returning to a standing position.
4. Level 3: Harness the power of celebration. Ask participants to squat down and stand up together five times. While going down and up, they repeat a word or phrase (for example, when they go down they say "Ooh," and when they go up they say "Ahh"). On each down and up, the group gets consistently louder until, on the last one, the group is yelling.

Processing

1. How did your movement on the webbing affect others?
2. How does your communication style affect others?
3. In a conflict, how can you help others?

Connections to Content: Use a racoon circle to gauge understanding. With the circle on the ground, prompt participants to step in and out of it in response to questions. (For instance, participants should move to the center of the circle if they can explain the plot of the story.) Try creating concentric circles of webbing, with the innermost circle representing meeting a learning target. Participants can see who needs more support and brainstorm how to help each other.

Social Awareness

Sometimes I wonder what the world would be like if every person on Earth shared a superpower that they have. What if we all respected differences and celebrated similarities? What if everyone thought about how others felt before they spoke or acted? What if everyone believed that everyone and everything has the right to be treated with kindness and respect?

What if labels were for jars and not for people? What if we all got to step into the shoes of the outcasts and the cool kids and got to reflect on what that feels like? What if every time there was conflict, we got into a circle and talked about it? What if we thought about how many people our waste could feed?

What if we thought of everyone as a potential friend? What if, when we returned home, we knew who we could ask for help? What if we all considered what makes a community and what we can do for them? What if we listened twice as much as we talked? What if our friendships defied social cliques? What if we took the time to learn more about our peers? What if, at the end of it all, we could appreciate each other for our strengths and for the times when we need support?

This vignette poses many questions about what the world could be like if we showed more empathy, appreciated more diversity, and practiced more kindness and respect. How could our actions change the world? While those big questions can be overwhelming, there are both small and large things that we can do to positively contribute to the world around us.

Social awareness is about recognizing the thoughts, feelings, and experiences of others. It includes gaining perspective, practicing empathy, respecting others, and appreciating diversity. Improving social awareness improves learning environments, because participants are more comfortable with a variety of perspectives and emotions, and they navigate conflict and differences with more positivity, which improves collaboration.

This section presents three themes: making connections, understanding one another, and exploring different perspectives. Even if participants know each other well, start with one of the first five activities before jumping into any of the others. Additionally, many of the activities at the beginning of this section can be incorporated into academic lessons to build interpersonal connections and subject-area knowledge simultaneously. Once participants are comfortable celebrating similarities and differences, you can continue to move sequentially through the lessons or pick a few to target specific skills or challenges in your classroom.

Categories

SEL Competency: Social Awareness

Objectives

- Participants will explore individual differences.
- Participants will demonstrate awareness of other people's perspectives.
- Participants will describe positive qualities in others.
- Participants will demonstrate respect for other people's perspectives.

Materials: None

Time: 15 minutes

Warm-Up: Brainstorm different categories of people as a group. Depending on your group, this simple prompt might offer an opportunity to introduce the concepts of categories, stereotypes, and biases. If there are already distinct social groupings or cliques within the larger group, start with a real example. For instance, there might be participants who play a varsity sport and those who do not. Use questions to help participants think about why categories, stereotypes, and biases exist.

Procedure

1. Participants will self-select into different categories by responding to a series of questions.

2. Ask the first question and ask participants to find the group that best represents them.

3. Once the groups have been formed, invite each group to speak loudly and clearly to announce the name of their category to the rest of their peers. The following is a list of possible categories:
   - When you cross your arms, which one is on top, your right or your left?
   - Which hand do you write with?
   - Which foot do you kick a ball with?
   - What is your favorite ice cream flavor?
   - Circle, square, triangle, or squiggle?
   - When do you shower?
   - What is your favorite class?
   - How many pets do you have?
   - North, South, East, or West?

Processing (Done in small groups of three to four participants)

1. Were you surprised by anything you learned about your peers? If so, what were those surprises?

2. What were some similarities you discovered between yourself and your peers that you did not already know?

3. How can our similarities and differences help us grow stronger as a group and community?

Connections to Content:

Language Arts: Compare yourself to a literary character.

Mathematics: Create a survey to learn more about the group, and graph the results.

Social Studies: Learn more about collective versus individualistic cultures.

Science: Learn more about the science of hand dominance.

Facilitation Tip: Processing in small groups may help quieter participants share more with peers.

Living Name Tags

SEL Competency: Social Awareness

Objectives

- Participants will explore individual differences.
- Participants will demonstrate awareness of other people's perspectives.
- Participants will describe positive qualities in others.
- Participants will demonstrate respect for other people's perspectives.

Materials: Name tags and markers

Time: 15–20 minutes

Warm-Up: Ask participants to sit comfortably and quietly. They may close their eyes or put their heads down if they'd like. Ask them to visualize themselves in an ideal vacation spot doing exactly what they want to be doing. Invite them to take three long, slow, deep breaths before bringing their attention back to the classroom. When they are ready, begin the activity.

Procedure

1. Ask participants to record the following information on their name tag: dream vacation destination (top), someone they look up to (middle), and favorite activity (bottom).

2. Ask participants to partner up with someone in the group whom they do not know very well. Each person takes a minute or two to share what they recorded on their name tag.

3. Have the participants take on the identity of the person they just learned about, and then change partners. They will share the name and information of the person they just learned about with a new partner.

4. Have participants sit or stand in a circle, and invite each participant to share one piece of new information that they learned about a peer during the activity.

Processing

1. By a show of fingers, how many pieces of new information did you learn about your peers?

2. Where do you all want to head for vacation? Why?

3. Who do you look up to? Why do you look up to them?

4. Were there any favorite activities that you would like to try? Any that you really don't like?

5. Why is it important to learn about the nonphysical characteristics of your peers? What are some barriers to learning about each other? What are some other ways to learn about each other?

 Connections to Content
Language Arts: Invite participants to write about a person they look up to and how they could be more like them.

Facilitation Tip: This activity can also provoke a conversation about rumors and gossip.

Find a New Spot

SEL Competency: Social Awareness

Objectives

- Participants will find similarities to make connections with their peers.
- Participants will practice strategies for building relationships with people who are different from themselves.
- Participants will recognize that others may experience situations differently from themselves.

Materials: Spot markers or chairs

Time: 15–20 minutes

Warm-Up: Share this Tom Robbins quote: "Our similarities bring us to a common ground; our differences allow us to be fascinated by each other." Ask participants to share their opinions about the quote.

Procedure

1. Use spot markers or chairs to form a large circle, with one fewer spot than the number of participants.
2. To start, each participant stands at a spot or sits in a chair and one person stands in the middle.
3. The person in the middle will finish the statement "Find a new spot if …" with something positive, nonphysical, and appropriate that applies to them.
4. If this statement also applies to other participants, those people move to a different spot in the circle, but not to the one on their immediate left or right. The person in the middle can claim a spot while the others are moving around.
5. The participant who is left without a spot stands in the middle and continues the game with another statement. Repeat Steps 3, 4, and 5 as long as desired.
6. The facilitator transitions to Level 2 by stepping into the middle and saying, "Find a new spot if you have ever had difficulty accepting someone new into a group."
7. During Level 2, remove an additional spot from the outside of the circle. The two participants in the middle of the circle now need to find a commonality (positive, nonphysical) and then tell peers, "Find a new spot if …"

Processing (continue using the spot markers)

1. Participants should find a new spot if they learned something new about a peer. Ask for volunteers to share their learning.

2. Participants should find a new spot if they were surprised during this activity. Ask for volunteers to share what surprised them.

3. Ask participants to construct two to three open-ended "Find a new spot if …" statements.

 Connections to Content: Use this activity true-or-false style to preview or review content, or use it to role-play characters from literature or history. For instance, "Find a new spot if you were in favor of this court decision."

Facilitation Tip: Being on the spot in the center of the circle can be overwhelming for some participants. As an alternative, use a unique spot (different color or different object) as part of the circle instead of using the middle.

Peek-a-Who?

SEL Competency: Social Awareness

Objectives

- Participants will practice strategies for building relationships with people who are different from themselves.
- Participants will identify each other by positive, nonphysical qualities.
- Participants will acknowledge the contributions of others.

Materials: Tarp or thick blanket, paper, and pens/pencils

Time: 20 minutes

Warm-Up: Play a quick round of Categories (p. 112), Commonalities (p. 122), or Find a New Spot (p. 116).

Procedure

1. Divide participants evenly into two groups.

2. The two groups sit on the floor with one group facing the other. There should be a space of 3 feet between the front rows of the groups.

3. Each group chooses one person to be "It." That person sits in front of the group facing the other group. (Demonstrate this.)

4. Level 1: The goal is to name the person who is in the front of the other group before they name you. The contestant is the only person who can speak in this round. The person who names that other person first wins that person for their team. (Demonstrate with two volunteers.) To make this more challenging, the groups are hidden behind a peek-a-who tarp or blanket. Raise the tarp between the two groups.

5. Groups pick their contestants. When both sides are ready, the facilitators holding the tarp say, "1-2-3 peek-a-who" and drop the tarp. One contestant will name the other first. Cheering ensues.

6. Play Level 1 a few times with different people being "It" in each round.

7. When groups demonstrate proficiency with the process and names, move to Level 2.

8. Level 2: With the tarp up, one person from each team is designated as "It" and sits in front of their group, but this time, the contestant faces their team rather than the tarp.

9. They are still responsible to name the person on the other side of the tarp, but can only do so by hearing about that person from their team. The team can describe the other contestant by their *positive* qualities (excluding all physical attributes). For example, sports a person plays, activities they are involved in, something they are good at, what they like to do, and nonphysical qualities like "friendly," "funny," etc.

10. Each contestant is saying names of people from the other group that might fit this description. As soon as the contestant says the correct name, the team should cheer so that the facilitator knows they are done.

11. Between rounds, pause and ask participants to share the positive qualities they said about the contestants.

12. If more people want to be contestants, put two from each team in front of the tarp. They are a team of two and must name both people from the other side before they can win.

13. Level 3 (optional): Contestants still cannot see and teammates are challenged to communicate with the contestant nonverbally.

Processing

1. By a show of fingers, how many new facts did you learn about your peers during this activity?

2. Individually or in small groups, write down different labels that you have used in the past to describe your peers or yourself. In a large group, sort the labels into physical and nonphysical characteristics.

3. Why is it challenging to avoid using physical characteristics?

4. With a partner, talk about labels your peers have used that you like and those that you dislike.

Connections to Content: Use a similar design to quiz participants on course content. Pose the question. In Level 1, the contestant just answers content-based questions. In Level 2, the contestant cannot see the question and teams must describe or provide hints verbally. In Level 3, teams must act out the answer.

Paper Airplanes

Note: Do not share the title of this activity with participants beforehand.

SEL Competency: Social Awareness

Objectives

- Participants will practice clear and effective communication skills.
- Participants will recognize that others may experience situations differently.

Materials: At least one sheet of 8½ x 11 inch paper for each participant

Time: 30 minutes

Warm-Up: Introduce the activity by talking to the group about communication. Note that it is such a routine part of our daily lives that we often take it for granted. We may find it hard to communicate in ways that are clear and easy for others to understand.

Procedure

1. Divide the class into pairs. One person in each pair will give instructions, and the other will receive them. Each pair should decide who will be the instructor and who will be the receiver.
2. Take all the instructors aside so the rest of the class can't overhear. Explain that they will be giving their partners step-by-step instructions on making a paper airplane, but they may not tell their partners what they are making.
3. Level 1: Instructors go back and sit with their backs to their partners. Give each partner a sheet of paper, explaining that they may do only what their instructor tells them to do and may not talk at all (no questions, no comments).
4. Pairs have 4–5 minutes to complete the task. When the time is up, invite pairs to compare their airplanes and discuss their successes or difficulties. Reverse roles and repeat.
5. Level 2: Receivers may ask questions and instructors may answer them.
6. Level 3: Repeat process with partners facing each other.

Processing

1. What was the difference between the first, second, and third attempts to follow the instructions to make the airplane?

2. What problems arose from not being able to ask questions? What were the advantages to being able to ask questions?

3. What was the easiest way to accomplish the task? Why?

4. How does this activity apply to our daily communication?

5. What happens when we fail to communicate clearly what we want?

Facilitation Tip: Add a test flight. Invite the architect of the plane that flew the farthest to teach the others how to build it—and then, of course, do another test flight.

Commonalities

SEL Competency: Social Awareness

Objectives

- Participants will find similarities with their peers.
- Participants will practice strategies for building relationships with people who are different from themselves.
- Participants will analyze how people from different groups can help one another and enjoy each other's company.

Materials: Paper and pens/pencils

Time: 15–20 minutes

Warm-Up: Ask participants to work individually to jot down a list of qualities they have in common with their peers. At the end of 1 minute, ask them to share how many commonalities are on their list. Ask for a few examples. Differentiate between nonphysical and physical characteristics. Discuss why it might be important to focus on nonphysical characteristics during this activity.

Procedure

1. Assemble participants in small groups (anywhere from two to eight people).
2. Give each group a piece of paper and a pen/pencil.
3. Each group is to generate a list of things that all members have in common but that are not obvious by looking at them (no physical characteristics).
4. Ask participants to set a goal of a certain number of commonalities that each group will identify or set a time period and see how many each group can come up with in that time.
5. Ask each group to share its list with the class.

Processing (in the same groups):

1. Did you hear any commonalities that your group shared with another group?
2. What was most difficult about developing your list of commonalities?
3. What was most helpful for developing the list of commonalities?

4. How can our similarities and differences help us grow stronger as a group and community?

Connections to Content: Invite participants to look for commonalities in your discipline. For instance, compare multiple characters from a short story, explore number patterns, or learn about plant and animal families.

FFEACH—Feelings Charades

Fast
Food,
Electrical
Appliances,
Cartoon
Heroes

SEL Competency: Social Awareness

Objectives

- Participants will practice describing feeling words.
- Participants will increase their emotional vocabulary.
- Participants will describe others' feelings in a variety of situations.
- Participants will demonstrate awareness of other people's emotions.

Materials: FFEACH Cards (p. 217) and Feelings Cards (p. 198)

Time: 30 minutes

Warm-Up: Spread out Feelings Cards and ask participants to choose one feeling they have felt in the past 24 hours. Invite sharing.

Procedure

1. Separate participants into groups of four or five and ask each group to sit in a different part of the room.

2. The goal of the activity is to successfully identify the words on as many FFEACH Cards as possible with the following rules:

   a. One person from each group will take a turn at a time.

   b. They will take a card from the central pile and look at it without showing it to anyone else in their group.

   c. The person will either act out the word or explain the word so their group can guess what feeling is written on their card.

   d. The person may not say any form of the word they are trying to act out (for example, for the word *helpless* they cannot use the word *help* to explain it) or tell them what it sounds like.

   e. If a team cannot guess the word, they may ask the facilitator for help or put the card back in the pile and try again.

   f. Once the word is guessed, the first person's turn is over and the next person draws a card.

   g. Everyone else on the team must take a turn before the first person may go again.

3. Each round continues for 5 minutes or until there are no cards remaining.

Processing

1. Invite participants to work collectively to sort the cards into easy, medium, and hard piles.

2. Invite participants to sort the cards using a different strategy.

3. Form trios and challenge them to share a time when they experienced an emotion in each of the easy, medium, and hard piles.

 Connections to Content: Use charades to preview or review course content.

Told by Fold

SEL Competency: Social Awareness

Objectives
Participants will analyze how their behavior may affect others.
Participants will identify ways to overcome misunderstandings.

Materials: Paper and pens/pencils

Time: 20 minutes

Warm-Up: Introduce the idea of *intent* versus *impact*. Sometimes our actions or behaviors do not lead to the consequence we expect. Sometimes our actions can cause misunderstandings. Invite participants to share a few examples.

Procedure

1. Give everyone a piece of paper and a pen/pencil.

2. Ask every participant to write a sentence. Let them know that their neighbor will draw their sentence and then they will draw their neighbor's.

3. Some participants may worry about their drawing ability. Assure them that someone *will* draw their sentence. It's okay to get silly—in fact, it's definitely more fun.

4. Participants pass the paper to the person next to them, and the receiver draws the sentence.

5. The receiver folds the paper over to cover the original sentence and passes the paper to the next participant with only the drawing showing.

6. The new participant writes a sentence to describe the drawing, folds the paper over the drawing, and hands the paper to the next participant with only the sentence showing. That participant draws the sentence, and so on.

7. At every pass, the paper will be folded from the last section. Allow as much time as you want at each pass, but momentum builds if each pass is under 3 minutes. Draw, pass, and write until the paper returns to the original author.

8. Reveal! Laughter should ensue.

Processing

1. Was this fun for you? Why or why not?

2. What is this phenomenon? We clearly started with one sentence; how did it evolve? We need to identify, clearly, *what* is happening.

3. Has something like this occurred to you before? Why do you think misunderstandings happen?

4. With a partner, brainstorm a way to resolve a misunderstanding after it happens and role-play for the group.

Connections to Content: Dive deeper into exploring multiple perspectives. For example, explain a variety of ways to solve mathematics problems, various routes to navigate from point A to point B on a map, alternative ways to test a hypothesis in science, or multiple narrative voices in a literary work.

Bodyguard

SEL Competency: Social Awareness

Objectives

- Participants will demonstrate consideration for others.
- Participants will identify ways to advocate for others.
- Participants will recognize how a situation would make them feel and modify their behaviors to treat others well.

Materials: Soft tossable objects, and Feelings Cards (p. 198) or other processing tool for warm-up

Time: 30 minutes

Warm-Up: Read a scenario that describes a group member being excluded from a team. Ask participants to brainstorm feelings they experience when they are left out. To scaffold understanding of emotions, use Feelings Cards or other visual-processing tools. Record the emotions that the participants name in order to revisit them during processing.

Procedure

1. Level 1: Participants form a large circle with one volunteer in the middle of the circle. Explain that the participants in the circle may not move. The participant in the middle of the circle may move but may not leave the area within the circle of participants. The goal of the challenge is for the participants standing in the circle to tag the participant in the middle of the circle with a tossable object (stress underhanded throws, and allow no throwing at the face). The participants in the circle may pass the objects to gain an easier tag. Switch the participant in the middle once they have been tagged.

2. Level 2: Assign a "bodyguard" to the participant in the middle of the circle. The bodyguard's goal is to protect the participant in the middle. The bodyguard can be tagged by the object, but once the "target" is tagged, a new pair enters the middle of the circle.

3. Level 3: Assign more than one bodyguard to the participant in the middle.

4. Level 4: Divide the class in half. One group picks one participant from their group whom they will protect. Explain that they can set up their protection anywhere in the classroom, in any configuration they'd like (while keeping it safe). The goal of the other group is to tag the person who is being protected by the other group. Depending on the ability of the participants and group size, each group can have offensive and defensive roles or you can play two rounds, switching the roles of the smaller groups.

Processing

1. What was it like to be in the circle? To be on the outside of the circle? To guard the person standing in the middle of the circle?

2. Does any of what happened remind you of real life? At home? At school?

3. If this does remind you of real life, is there anything you can take away from the activity that might help you navigate at school or home?

4. If they haven't been mentioned by participants, introduce the terms *bully*, *target*, *ally*, and *bystander*. Ask for participants to raise their hands if they have ever felt like a target, an ally, or a bystander.

5. Bring in the vocabulary from the warm-up brainstorm: What did it feel like to be a bully? Target? Ally? Bystander?

 Connections to Content

Mathematics: Connect the number of hits versus the number of protectors to probability or rate.

Science: Discuss the risks and benefits of animals being solitary or herd creatures.

Poker Face

SEL Competency: Social Awareness

Objectives

- Participants will analyze ways in which their behavior may affect other people's feelings and adjust that behavior accordingly.
- Participants will distinguish between bullying and non-bullying situations.
- Participants will explain how individual, social, and cultural differences may increase vulnerability to bullying and then identify ways to address it.

Materials: A deck of playing cards

Time: 30 minutes

Warm-Up: Brainstorm places where participants gather in groups. What rules guide interactions in those places?

Procedure

1. Hand each participant a playing card and tell them not to look at it.
2. Ask them to place the card facing out on their forehead and stress the importance of not trying to find out the suit or number of the card on their head.
3. Ask the participants to form groups based on their cards (without looking at their own).
4. After the designated amount of time has expired, have participants arrange themselves in order according to the rank of card they think they have on their forehead.
5. When everyone feels like they are in the correct order, they can take their card down and look at their actual rank.
6. Do a few rounds during which they imagine they are in the places they listed in the brainstorm. For instance, does a different hierarchy exist in the lunchroom than in an auditorium?

Processing

1. Redistribute cards and have participants form groups based on the suit of their cards.

    a. Hearts make a list of feelings they felt during the activity.

    b. Clubs make a list of groups that exist in their community.

    c. Diamonds make a list of positive things that can happen when you hang out with the same people most of the time.

    d. Spades make a list of negative things that can happen when you hang out with the same people most of the time.

2. How did this activity remind you of real life?

3. Do you witness people being excluded in your community? Why are people being excluded?

4. What does it feel like to be left out? What is wrong with leaving others out?

5. What would your community be like if more people were included than excluded?

6. What can you say or do to be more inclusive of others?

7. Define bullying and discuss the policies that exist in your community.

 Connections to Content

Language Arts: Have participants compare themselves to a literary character, using both physical and nonphysical characteristics.

Community Maps

SEL Competency: Social Awareness

Objectives

- Participants will explore a community need and generate possible solutions.
- Participants will demonstrate a desire to contribute to the well-being of their community.
- Participants will demonstrate a desire to contribute to the well-being of their school.
- Participants will discuss community, both local and global.

Materials: Large paper and markers

Time: 30–45 minutes

Warm-Up: Present a few examples of maps and invite participants to brainstorm map characteristics. Ask participants to write or draw about what community means to them.

Procedure

1. Divide participants into groups of three or four and give them 10–15 minutes to draw a map of their community on the paper. Try not to specify what type of community, as this is where the majority of the processing comes into play.
2. Set up a gallery walk so all participants have an opportunity to see all maps.

Processing

1. Challenge participants to find three to five similarities and three to four differences in the maps.
2. With a partner, discuss what those overlapping and distinct characteristics might mean.
3. What is at the center of the maps? What are some of the important parts of the communities?
4. What might be missing from the maps? Are they also missing from the communities?

5. What are some tangible ways that we can continue to build our classroom community? School community? Local community?

Connections to Content

Language Arts: Write an Autobiographical Poem (p. 194).

Mathematics: Explore budgets. What does it cost to run a school? A city? A family?

Social Studies: What resources are available to help people in your community? How can you help fill a community need?

Science: Investigate what animals live in our communities.

Mirage

SEL Competency: Social Awareness

Objectives
- Participants will verbalize three behaviors of an active listener.
- Participants will explain how they know someone is listening to them.

Materials: Toothpicks

Time: 15 minutes

Warm-Up: Review LEADSTAR (p. 5) before introducing this activity.

Procedure
1. Pair up participants, then give each participant five toothpicks.
2. Explain to the participants that each of them will get the chance to make something with their toothpicks. One partner explains what they are making, the other partner must listen, not talk, and build what they hear.
3. Partners switch roles.
4. You can increase the challenge by allowing the listener to ask *one* question.

Processing
1. How could you tell your partner was listening?
2. What components of effective communication were helpful?
3. What are some qualities or behaviors of an *active* listener? How is the listener involved in the conversation?
4. What makes it difficult to communicate with a partner?
5. How can we improve our communication with each other?

Bird's Nest

SEL Competency: Social Awareness

Objectives

- Participants will engage in the planning phase of collaboration.
- Participants will practice verbal and nonverbal communication.
- Participants will work together to create a freestanding structure that will support a golf ball.

Materials: 3 feet of masking tape, twenty sheets of newspaper, and one golf ball (one set per group)

Time: 45 minutes

Warm-Up: Introduce or review the ABCDE (Ask, Brainstorm, Choose, Do, and Evaluate) model of problem solving. If your school or organization uses a different problem-solving model, feel free to use it instead.

Procedure

1. Divide group into teams of three to four participants and distribute materials.

2. Using only the materials provided, each team must build the tallest freestanding structure possible that will support the weight of a golf ball.

3. Present a time schedule such as:

3 minutes—plan
5 minutes—build
3 minutes—plan
5 minutes—build
2 minutes—plan
5 minutes—build
_____
23 minutes—total time

4. During the planning phase, participants may speak, but they may not touch the materials.

5. During the building phase, participants may not speak.

Processing

1. Are all group members happy with the results?

2. If you could make a list of strengths and improvements regarding your team's communication and collaboration skills, what would be on the list?

3. Was it helpful to not talk during the building phase?

4. How can words sometimes affect our ability to work collaboratively?

5. Does your structure symbolize anything to you? If so, what?

 Connections to Content: Incorporate a similar planning and building/working structure in class. If participants have discrete time to plan versus respond, does the finished product look different?

Responsible Decision Making

During my week at the Leadership School, I gradually came to know my classmates and cabinmates. At first, we focused on name tags and silly questions that actually helped me learn new things about my classmates that I wouldn't have discovered back at school. I felt the same way when we played group games like Hula Hoop Pass and Group Juggle which pushed us to talk about decision making and work with people we don't usually interact with. These activities helped me see my classmates in a different light and made me realize that we could support each other even if we are not all close friends.

We learned about healthy risk taking and comfort zones. During the day, we did a lot of problem-solving activities with our classmates. I had the hardest time not getting frustrated, but I got better every day. We talked about having a growth mind-set a lot during our team-building challenges. One day, we did an activity on the low ropes course where we all had to swing to a platform and stand together. At first, we were all shouting out our ideas and then we realized we needed to take turns and listen to each other. Then it was much easier to solve the challenge.

In the cabin, at first, I was nervous to be sharing a bunk bed and bathrooms with people I had never talked to before. The first night, my cabin educator welcomed us and made the night so much fun with games of Apples to Apples and Mafia that I got comfortable without even realizing it. The last night was my favorite; each cabin worked together and planned a skit or a dance to perform in front of all the other cabins. The last morning was filled with hugs, some tears, and promises to talk over the weekend and hang out when we were back at school.

On Monday, I had been so nervous I felt like I wouldn't be able to make it through the week away from home. By Friday, I couldn't believe the week was over and found myself wishing we didn't have to leave. I feel so lucky for the time I spent at Kieve. I know my friends and I will be talking about this experience for a while.

Learning through experience is a valuable process that requires reflection on what works and what doesn't work. In this vignette, you can follow the participant's thought process throughout the week. In the moment something might not be going well, but when they take the time to stop and reevaluate, they learn from the experience.

Responsible decision making includes healthy risk taking, creative problem solving, and reflecting on experiences in order to learn and grow. Whether working alone or with others, it's about the process of making informed choices. Decision making is a life skill with both immediate application and long-term benefits and consequences.

While all of the activities in this book encourage reflection and inherently build decision-making skills, this section focuses on them specifically. The section begins with three activities to isolate key components of the decision-making process: goal setting, choice, and influence. The next five activities highlight the role of personal choices in decision making, and the last five activities focus on group decision making.

Hula Hoop Pass

SEL Competency: Responsible Decision Making

Objectives

- Participants will practice effective communication.
- Participants will work together to meet a goal.

Materials: Hula hoops or rope loops and a stopwatch

Time: 25 minutes

Warm-Up: If participants have not held hands with each other before, ask them to hold hands and pass a hand-squeeze pulse around the circle.

Procedure

1. Ask the group to form a circle holding hands. Ask two people to let go of their grip long enough to place their hands through a hula hoop before rejoining them.
2. The group's task is to pass the hula hoop around the circle in a specified direction until it returns to the starting point.

3. Once they have passed the hoop once around the circle, ask them to set a goal for how quickly they can send the hula hoop around the circle again. Time their next pass around the circle. Repeat as many times as desired (setting new time goals before each pass).

4. If your group would like an added level of difficulty, use two hula hoops and send them around the circle in opposite directions.

Processing

1. What were some challenges of this activity?
2. How did the group come up with a plan?
3. Did you use the same plan the entire time or switch to a new strategy partway through?
4. Did you have to alter your goal to make it harder or more accessible?
5. In real life, do we make goals that are either too easy or too challenging?

 Connections to Content: Use this activity as an introduction to an activity that has many paths to the outcome. It can also be helpful when a group or individual is struggling to see alternative solutions to a problem or understand multiple perspectives.

Facilitation Tip: Participants may need some prompting partway through the activity when working on how to shorten their time. It can help to remind them, "If you want to take a break and talk about a plan, that's fine." This encourages them to take a step back from the activity and reevaluate, rather than repeating the same strategy over and over. Alternatively, you could frontload this activity by reviewing the use of a STOP call (p. 65).

Depending on the age and maturity of participants, you may find that some participants are uncomfortable holding hands. This could be a great time to address this, or you can adapt by adding extra "teammates" between them. For example, if Charlie and Annie are refusing to hold hands, you could put a small stuffed animal between them. Then they can each hold on to the animal, connecting the circle without needing to physically touch.

That Person Over There

SEL Competency: Responsible Decision Making

Objectives

- Participants will practice clear and effective communication.
- Participants will experience the opportunity of telling someone else's story.

Materials: Image cards or open-ended photos or objects

Time: 15–20 minutes

Warm-Up: Play a quick game of Telephone (p. 7) or Movement Telephone (in which you copy movements from person to person).

Procedure

1. Lay out large-image side of image cards or other processing tool and ask participants to select one in response to a prompt. (For example, "Choose a card that reminds you of your favorite book.")
2. Ask participants to share their choice with a peer. ("I chose this card because …")
3. After they share their reasoning, they swap cards.
4. Then that partner shares the story with a different partner by saying, "That person over there, [NAME], chose this card because …" and then swap cards again with someone new.
5. Each time the card is passed, the original owner's story is shared.
6. Ask participants to return to their seats when they have received their own card back.
7. Have participants share their original story as well as the revision they heard in the final swap.

Processing

1. How did the stories change over time? Why?
2. How did it feel to have someone else tell "your story"?
3. How does this relate to real life?

Connections to Content: Use a similar method to preview or review content by choosing a prompt specific to your topic area. For instance, in science, ask participants to choose a vocabulary term, define it, and then pass along the definition. Share the information in summary at the end of the activity (Step 7 above) so you can address any misconceptions or misinformation.

Facilitation Tip: Repeating the story in the first person shifts the focus of this activity to make it more about gaining perspective and building empathy.

Inchworm

SEL Competency: Responsible Decision Making

Objectives

- Participants will practice effective communication.
- Participants will explore how external factors influence decision making.

Materials: None

Time: 20–30 minutes

Warm-Up: If participants have not held hands with each other before, begin with a hand-squeeze pulse around the circle (or modify the activity to limit hand holding, see p. 141).

Procedure

1. Divide the group in half to create two teams.
2. Team members connect hands to create two inchworms.
3. Explain that one end of each inchworm has to be in contact with a stable object at all times (something 15 feet or higher, such as a tree, a corner of a building, etc.).
4. The team cannot move until the loose end of the inchworm makes contact with another stable object.
5. The team that makes it to the final object in the fewest number of moves wins.
6. The destinations can be the same distance, but the teams should start from different ends.

Processing

1. How did the group know if the opposite end of the inchworm made it to an object?
2. Which components of effective communication were helpful during the activity?
3. How did external factors influence the path you chose?
4. What are some examples of external factors that affect your decisions in everyday life?

 Connections to Content: Use the activity to highlight the importance of prerequisite skills and knowledge. Point out that, just like moving across the inchworm course, there are checkpoints in academic areas.

Group Juggle

SEL Competency: Responsible Decision Making

Objectives

- Participants will consider the ways in which routine decisions are interconnected.
- Participants will practice effective communication.
- Participants will evaluate how external factors and risky behavior impact decision making and performance.

Time: 45 minutes

Materials: Ten to fifteen soft tossable objects

Warm-Up: Ask participants to list five things that are important in their daily life.

Procedure

1. Give the group the following rules:

   a. The object has to return to the facilitator but has to go to everyone in the circle first.

   b. No one can have it twice.

   c. No one can pass it to the person on their immediate left or right.

   d. The object must be passed underhand.

2. Toss one object to a participant across the circle from you.

3. After the group has established an order, pass the object around in the same order a couple of times to solidify the order firmly in everyone's mind.

4. Ask participants to name things that are important in their life (family, friends, sports, etc.)

5. Assign objects to represent the important parts of their lives.

6. Tell the group that the objective is to get all of the objects around the circle in the same order you send them out, dropping them as little as possible. (This serves as a representation of someone's "life" and what it might be like to juggle all of its parts and keep it under control.)

7. Toss the first object, wait a couple of tosses, and then toss the second object, then the third, and so on. Get all of the objects in circulation before the first one comes back to you.

8. Pause and ask the group to describe the way this "life" is going. Ask them to describe in one or two words what it is like to try to keep everything under control and moving smoothly.

9. Ask the group to list some risky behaviors that someone might try in order to make their life "better."

10. Introduce an object or two that represent risky behaviors. Give the risky objects a different passing path or other specific role (for example, it can't be thrown, it must bounce once, etc.).

11. Allow at least two rounds with the risky behavior in the mix before moving to processing.

Processing

1. What was challenging during this activity?

2. What strategies did you use to try to meet the goal?

3. Were you successful? Why or why not?

4. If you were to redo this challenge, what would you change? Why?

5. How does this activity represent an average day in your life?

 ### Connections to Content

Language Arts: Help participants break down a lengthy assignment into stages.

Mathematics: Discuss ways to check work along the way.

Social Studies: Invite a guest speaker to introduce a local social issue and steps that are being taken to address it.

Science: Examine the environmental impact of our daily decisions.

Facilitation Tip: This activity sequences well with Warp Speed (p. 60). You can increase the chaos by requiring participants to move around the space for the duration of the round.

Steal the Bacon

SEL Competency: Responsible Decision Making

Objectives

- Participants will practice healthy risk taking.
- Participants will consider how external factors affect decision making.

Materials: Portable object to steal that won't fit in your pocket (the "bacon"), and pen/pencil and paper for warm-up

Time: 20–30 minutes

Warm-Up: Ask participants to write down a personal goal on a piece of paper. Let them know that they will revisit the goal after the activity.

Procedure

1. Participants stand at one end of an open space, shoulder to shoulder in a line. It's helpful to mark off a line for them to stand behind (for example, a rope, a line in the sand, the place where the pavement meets the dirt, etc.).
2. Stand at the other end of the open space, facing them with the object lying on the ground a few feet in front of you.
3. Challenge participants to work together to retrieve the object and return it to their side of the line.

4. When you are facing the group, all participants must be frozen.

5. When you are standing with your back turned to the group, the participants may move.

6. If you turn around to face the group and see someone moving, that person needs to return to the start line.

7. The object needs to be passed from person to person—it cannot be thrown.

8. If you turn around to face the group and the object is gone, you can guess who has it three times before turning around again. If you guess correctly, they return the object and go back to the starting line. If you guess incorrectly, you turn around and they continue toward their end with the object.

Processing

1. What was the goal of this activity? Was there a plan?

2. Did everyone know the plan? Did you all agree with it?

3. What are some risky decisions that you made during the activity?

4. What influenced your decisions and risk taking during this activity?

5. What factors influence your decisions and risk taking every day?

6. How does taking risks affect your progress toward your personal and group goals?

7. Think about the personal goal that you wrote down at the beginning. Do you have a plan to reach that goal? Does it include healthy risk taking?

 Connections to Content: This activity reminds participants that there are steps along the way to success. It can also highlight when there are communication breakdowns within a group. The group will gain cohesion trying to take the object from the facilitator.

Facilitation Tip: Some groups will struggle to work collaboratively to complete this task and need to revisit it multiple times. For other groups, you may need to make it more difficult. You can add levels of difficulty by increasing the number of objects, limiting the number of touches by group members, and decreasing the length of time your back is turned.

Stepping Stones

SEL Competency: Responsible Decision Making

Objectives
- Participants will practice effective communication.
- Participants will work together to solve a problem.

Materials: Two boundary ropes, and "stepping stones" (wooden blocks for 3D; paper plates, kickboards, or spot markers for 2D)

Time: 20 minutes

Warm-Up: Ask participants to reflect on whether they prefer to work individually or in a group and why.

Procedure
1. Set up boundary ropes to clearly mark a beginning and an end.
2. Explain that, as a group, participants must travel from Point A to Point B, using only the "stepping stones."
3. Stones can be swapped and shared, but cannot be shuffled along the ground.
4. Participants must always have their feet on a stone; they cannot step onto the ground itself.
5. If a participant touches the ground with any part of their body, they must return to the start.
6. If a participant loses contact with a stone, it is taken away by the facilitator.
7. The goals are to get everyone across and to retain as many stones as possible.

Processing
1. What was the original plan to get across? Did that plan change?
2. Was everyone informed of the plan and any changes that followed?
3. What was the importance of communication within this challenge?
4. What obstacles did the group face along the way?
5. How did individual decisions impact the success of the group?

Connections to Content: The experience of having a stone taken away from the group is a powerful metaphor that can be connected to classroom experiences. By considering use of materials, class time lost due to distractions, or the importance of a small but necessary piece of information, participants can think about how to help themselves and each other to be successful in the classroom.

Facilitation Tip: Often the physical layout of this activity leads to many individuals with many ideas and only a little listening. You can highlight this by recording key phrases you hear during the challenge and sharing them with the group during processing.

The Maze

SEL Competency: Responsible Decision Making

Objectives
- Participants will practice making decisions on their own.
- Participants will discuss peer influence on choices.

Time: 20 minutes

Materials: 25 spot markers or paper plates, and paper and pens/pencils for warm-up

Warm-Up: Ask participants to write down all of the decisions they have made during the past 24 hours. Then ask them to rank those decisions from 1 to 5 (with 1 being an automatic and quick decision and 5 the most deliberate and thoughtful decision).

Procedure
1. Arrange the spots in any pattern you like to make the maze.
2. Have participants form a circle around the maze.
3. Explain that the object is for each person to find the correct path through the maze.
4. Ask the participant standing closest to the starting area to step onto a dot in the first row that they think is part of the solution.
5. If the participant makes their own choice of which dot to move to, then they are prompted to continue.
6. If the participant steps based on someone else's influence, the facilitator will interrupt the participant by saying "Stop" and they should return to the end of the line to try again. The next participant in line begins their turn, using what they learned from the previous try or tries.
7. The problem has been solved when each group member has made it independently through the maze.

Processing
1. What skills did the group need to utilize in order to find the solution to the problem?
2. How were people making decisions about where to step next?

3. Did anyone feel peer pressure to step on a spot that they did not want to step on? How did you handle that peer pressure?

4. Was this problem difficult? Is life ever difficult? If so, how?

5. Did this problem have anything to do with risky behaviors?

6. Do people ever influence others to make a decision that may be incorrect for them? Why?

7. How can you become a better decision maker?

8. What skills do you need to help make decisions that are right for you?

Variation: Prior to beginning, create a set solution. Instead of emphasizing independent decision making, challenge the group to find the solution together.

 Connections to Content: This activity can be helpful if participants are having trouble working independently. The "think aloud" version can help participants strengthen their metacognition.

Facilitation Tip: As the facilitator, it can be difficult to judge whether choices are made independently. Ask participants to "think aloud" during the activity to help identify peer influence.

Facilitation Tip: Spotting

Many of the following activities require students to be competent spotters. Please teach (or review) safe spotting technique before beginning any activity that calls for spotting.

Spotting is the means of safeguarding an individual during low elements and initiatives when participants are relatively close to the ground or on the ground. The main role of the spotter is to support and protect the head and upper-body area (particularly the spinal cord) from injury if the participant falls. Spotters don't necessarily prevent the fall, but they reduce the likelihood of injury.

Two rules of spotting

1. Always **pay attention**: The spotter must always watch the participant.

2. Always **be ready**: The spotter must always be ready with hands up.

Suggested support stance for spotters

Surfer Stance: Feet shoulder width apart, one leg back from the other with foot turned out and knees slightly bent.

Bumpers Up: Arms up, slightly bent with hands open. (Hands and fingers should be in the shape of *spoons* rather than *forks*.)

Notes

1. The spotter needs to be close to the participant and follow all their movements.

2. The spotter needs to be ready to come into physical contact with the participant if a fall occurs.

3. The spotter needs to understand their responsibility, and group members need to trust one another.

Spotting communication

1. Communication among the group members should be consistent and clear.

2. Although the actual words of spotting communication vary according to the activity and the participants involved, there should always be a system of check and response before the activity begins. A sample communication sequence includes:

    a. Check: Climber asks, "Ready?" or "Spotters Ready?"

    b. Confirmation: Spotters respond, "Ready."

c. Double Check: Climber states the activity, "Climbing" or "Leaning."

d. Confirmation: Spotters respond, "Climb!" or "Lean!"

3. At the end of the activity, spotters must stay engaged until they hear the participant say "Safe" or "I am safe."

Spotting practice

Two-Person Mirroring: As one person moves, the partner duplicates or shadows every move.

Stand Off: Partners stand facing each other with their own feet together and try to knock each other off balance by striking palms against one another.

Squat Thrust: Partners assume a precarious balanced position by squatting opposite one another (balancing on the balls of the feet) and try to knock each other off balance by striking palms against one another. (Try it in slow motion for a more cooperative experience.)

Tower of Feetsa

SEL Competency: Responsible Decision Making

Objectives

- Participants will collaborate to reach a goal.
- Participants will build trust and communicate needs throughout the activity.
- The group will assess themselves and try to attain a higher goal.

Materials: String, sheets of paper, or other measuring device

Time: 40 minutes

Warm-Up: Ask participants to define trust. Ask participants to share, with a partner, an example of a trustworthy peer or adult and describe the qualities that make someone trustworthy. Additionally, if participants are not familiar with spotting techniques, run a spotting primer before doing this activity (p. 154).

Procedure

1. Explain to participants that this will be a trust activity. The goal is to create the highest tower of feet possible, while keeping everyone safe.
2. The tower of feet must start at the ground. The feet must be touching heel to toe. Participants may only have one foot in the tower. No outside props may be used.
3. Participants who are not touching the ground must have at least two spotters. Remind participants of the importance of keeping everyone safe.
4. Once the rules have been explained, the team may plan and make their first attempt.
5. Once the first attempt has been measured and recorded, the group can assess whether or not they would like to try a second attempt.

Processing

1. Was there a clear plan?
2. Did everyone agree with the plan? Why or why not?
3. How can trust make it easier to agree with a plan?
4. What can the group gain from this experience?

Connections to Content

Language Arts: Discuss the elements that provide structure in a piece of writing and how they work together.

Mathematics: Identify which shapes are most stable for construction and why.

Social Studies: Develop a plan for creating positive community change.

Science: Discuss the laws of physics that were involved while creating the Tower of Feetsa.

How High?

SEL Competency: Responsible Decision Making

Objectives

- Participants will collaborate to set and reach a realistic goal.
- Participants will consider safety and consequences of decisions.
- Participants will consider feedback from others on the decision-making process.

Materials: Chalk or masking tape

Time: 40 minutes

Warm-Up: Review the SMART goal model, with an emphasis on achievable, realistic, and timely. If participants are not familiar with spotting techniques, run a spotting primer before doing this activity (p. 154).

Procedure

1. The task is to put a chalk mark or piece of masking tape at the highest point in a designated area during the allotted time.
2. Everyone must agree on the plan and participate in the task.

Processing

1. Was the goal realistic?
2. Did you reach the goal? Why or why not?
3. Are all goals realistic for every person?
4. Can you give an example of a time when someone else set an unrealistic goal for you?
5. Have you ever set an unrealistic goal for yourself?
6. How is goal setting connected to emotions?

 Connections to Content: Encourage participants to set daily, weekly, and monthly goals in your content area.

Facilitation Tip: Despite the simple procedures, this activity is challenging. Being open to interpretation while requiring agreement of the group for success creates a flexible and effective challenge. If you are having trouble finding the right level of difficulty for your group, using activities with fewer instructions allows the group to create the challenge level through their interpretations of the task.

Over Under Through

SEL Competency: Responsible Decision Making

Objectives
- Participants will face a problem together and work through it as a cooperative unit.
- Participants will gain trust in one another by relying on their peers.
- Participants will understand the importance of positive risk taking.
- Participants will realize the importance of individual roles and personal responsibility.
- Participants will identify assertive behavior and explain how it made a difference in the outcome.

Materials: Webbing, rope, or string (enough to hang at three heights)

Time: 55 minutes

Warm-Up: Participants must learn the skill of "levitation" first:

1. One leader and eight lifters will be in place for a standard trust lean.
2. The leader is in charge of the head, neck, and all communication that will take place.
3. Two participants will be in charge of each of the following: shoulders, lower back, upper legs, and feet.
4. Participants should be lifted in the supine position, faceup.
5. When lifting fellow participants, it is especially important to support the neck and head.
6. If passing a participant through an object, pass them feet first.
7. The remaining participants will circle the levitation and stand in a spotting position.
8. The leader will then guide the team in a levitation.
9. Participant will lie in a supine position while the rest of the team gets in position to lift them up.
10. The leader is in charge and will give all the necessary instructions.
11. The participant is raised to waist level by the lifters in zippered position holding their head, shoulders, hips, and legs.
12. The leader will ask if the participant wants to go higher, eventually up to about 5 feet.

161

13. The leader will also direct the participant to be brought back to the ground.

14. Once the participant is at waist level again, the feet will slowly be lowered and the head raised, until the participant can stand freely on their own and says "Safe" or "I am safe."

If participants are not comfortable and successful in safe levitation, DO NOT proceed with this activity.

Procedure

1. Once the group has a clear understanding of levitation, divide the team into two smaller groups. One small team stands on each side of the ropes. The ropes should be positioned so that the top rope is about 4¾ feet off the ground, the middle is about 3½ feet, and the bottom is about 1½ feet. The goal is to get every member of each team to the other side.

2. The small groups on either side must work together to pass people through in the following pattern:

a. Over (over the top rope)

b. Under (under the bottom rope)

c. Through (above the middle rope and under the top rope)

3. The pattern is continuous. The two groups must alternate passing someone through, so if one side passes someone over, the other side must send someone under. The activity is finished when all participants are on the opposite side from which they began.

4. Explain to participants that if someone touches the rope on their way through, they must go back. If a lifter from the outside touches the rope, the person being lifted must return to their starting place. It is important to ensure that all levitations are performed faceup and head first, with at least six people on either side.

Processing

1. What were some examples of assertiveness and clear, effective communication that you witnessed during the challenge? How did it make a difference?

2. Did people speak up about how they wanted to get through or help? Did anyone end up with a role that they were uncomfortable with?

3. What were some of the ways you observed the group unite toward a common goal? What were some of the ways that the groups created more obstacles?

4. Do people limit themselves in your school? How?

5. What are some of the real-life consequences of following the crowd and not creating change? What is a consequence of thinking you can't make a difference?

6. What might you change if you could do this challenge again?

Responsible
Decision Making

Lifelines

SEL Competency: Responsible Decision Making

Objectives

- Participants reflect on their life story while sharing goals for the future.
- Participants find commonalities and points of intersection between their lives.

Time: 30 minutes

Materials: Large paper and markers

Warm-Up: Show an example of a timeline from an age-appropriate text. Explore which events are labeled on the timeline and ask how events are chosen to be included. Encourage participants to think of two to three events in their life that meet that criteria before beginning the activity.

Procedure

1. Divide participants into four small groups and give each group one piece of paper. Each individual member of the group should choose a marker in a different color.
2. Ask each group to draw one timeline, on which all group members will mark dates of their major life moments in the past, present, and future.
3. Participants choose the start and end dates of their group's timeline. (The phrasing here is up to the facilitator. Participants should feel free to creatively depict their timelines, beyond just a straightforward line down the page.)
4. Give the groups 15–20 minutes to create their timelines. When they are done and waiting for other groups to finish, encourage them to think about the overlaps between each other's lives, add major world events that they remember or anticipate, or add illustrations.
5. After all the groups have finished, have a gallery walk to share the timelines.

Processing

1. What did you put on your timeline and why?
2. What are the events that we remember most? Are they positive or negative?

3. Was it a risk to put something more serious or personal on the timeline? When do we take risks in sharing? Are the risks worth it?

4. What did you learn about each other? About the group?

5. How do we share our life stories and pasts with one another?

6. What do you want to see on your future timeline?

7. How do your current decisions impact your future lives?

 Connections to Content: Explore career paths that connect with each academic content area. Host a guest speaker with a career in your content area or invite participants to browse job postings that require the same skills they are working on in the classroom.

Facilitation Tip: This activity is helpful for learning more about a new group, or breaking down boundaries and finding commonalities in a well-established group.

Peace Treaty

SEL Competency: Responsible Decision Making

Objectives

- Participants will analyze why both parties in a conflict feel the way they do.
- Participants will evaluate how relationships influence group decision making.
- Participants will paraphrase conflicting perspectives of parties in a conflict.

Materials: None

Time: 10–30 minutes

Warm-Up: Talk a bit about cause and effect: "If you do this, then this will happen." Invite participants to share examples relevant to their lives. If compromise or conflict come up, preview those two terms.

Procedure

1. Divide participants into four groups. Situate the groups opposite each other to form the corners of a square.
2. Invite each group to huddle up and pick some sort of sign that everyone is able to do and that will represent their group. Offer examples like fingers on heads as antennae or "I'm a little teapot" handle and spout.
3. Once each group has decided on their sign, they show their signs to the other groups so everyone can see and try every other sign.
4. The facilitator explains that when they say "1-2-3-show," each group has to throw a sign. They need to decide beforehand which sign they will throw as a group. It can be any group's sign—it does *not* have to be their own.
5. The goal is for all four groups to come to agreement and throw the same sign, but there can be no communication between groups while each group is deciding which sign to throw.
6. Repeat Step 4 until successful or out of time.

Processing

1. Ask participants to reflect individually by writing or drawing about what happened.

167

2. While still in groups, discuss how you decided which signs to throw. Why? One group member should report to the whole class.

3. What did you notice the other groups do?

4. What emotions did you feel during the activity? Why?

5. What similarities do you see between what happened here and how groups at school (or in the world) make decisions?

 ### Connections to Content

Language Arts: Read about a conflict and discuss how it could have been resolved differently.

Mathematics: Discuss averages (mean, median, and mode) and what they reveal about a larger group of data.

Science: Discuss the scientific method and the ways in which scientists make decisions.

Social Studies: Explore voting and democracy or other forms of government. Discuss how large groups of people make decisions.

Facilitation Tip: Often there will be at least one group that refuses to acquiesce and throw another group's signs and just continues to throw their own. This is okay. It is perfectly fine if the peace treaty just doesn't happen. It's good fodder for the debrief. Sometimes the peace treaty happens fairly quickly. That is also good fodder.

Pass the Can

SEL Competency: Responsible Decision Making

Objectives

- Participants will work collaboratively to complete a challenge.
- Participants will practice clear and effective communication.

Materials: Large can or bucket

Time: 30–45 minutes

Warm-Up: If using for content review, ask group to write content-area questions and put them in the can.

Procedure

1. Participants stand or sit in a circle.

2. Ask them to pass the can around the circle.

3. After the first round, invite participants to develop rules for each subsequent round.

4. The challenge in this activity comes from the rules that the group develops.

Processing

1. Did the group have a plan? Did you follow it?

2. Did a leader emerge?

3. What was difficult about the challenge?

4. Did anyone get frustrated? Why? How did you deal with frustration?

5. What would you do differently if you needed to do the challenge again?

 Connections to Content: Put preview or review content questions in the can. If they fall out, participants need to answer them.

Facilitation Tip: The materials that you use for an activity can help frame it. You could frontload the activity by putting goals or another meaningful object in the can so it needs to stay upright.

Processing the Experience

Each activity in this book is framed to address particular social-emotional learning competencies; however, the magic of experiential learning is that it is dynamic, and participants learn through both the action and reflection. From scaffolding reflection skills to providing alternative questions and processing tools, this chapter will help you build your processing toolbox.

Participants who have never taken time to think about their learning often need to learn and practice how to process their experiences effectively. Frontloading, answering questions in small groups, and participant-directed processing are ways to help build reflection skills. Answering questions in a large group and reflecting independently, especially in writing, take more time and practice to master. That said, there are four primary ways to categorize processing methods: frontloading, question-and-answer processing, participant-directed processing, and independent reflection.

Frontloading happens before the activity starts, through framing or briefing as instructions are given. The facilitator primes the participants for the activity by revisiting, reminding, highlighting, and discussing group behaviors. The warm-ups frontload each activity by encouraging groups to brainstorm ideas, demonstrate prerequisite skills, or model expectations. If a group has developed a set of norms or classroom expectations, the facilitator can frontload the experience by reminding the group of those norms or expectations. Because frontloading is driven by the facilitator, it is often the easiest type of processing to begin with for both the facilitators and participants.

For the second step, **question-and-answer processing**, each activity listed in this book includes processing questions that the facilitator can ask participants to respond to in a large group or in small-group discussions. Traditional question-and-answer processing typically happens after the activity is completed. However, like the formative assessments used in most classrooms, questions may be even more powerful when they are posed during an activity. The typical sequence of inquiry can be simplified to the following questions: "What?" "So what? "And now what?"

The prompts provided near the end of each activity description offer one example of how to reflect on and process the experience. However, you may find that the participants are better prepared to have a different conversation.

For instance, you may have chosen to facilitate Group Juggle to provoke a conversation about decision making and instead the participants are engaging in conversation about planning ahead. As the facilitator, you can choose to redirect the conversation back to decision making or you can engage in the conversation about planning ahead. The Alternative Processing Themes and Questions provide questions and prompts around a variety of topics. You may want to flag that page so you can reference it quickly when your group is exploring something different that emerged from the experience than you were anticipating.

The third category is **participant-directed processing**. It typically occurs after the activity when the facilitator provides a means of open-ended reflection. Participants then guide the reflective process through the use of actions, props, and/or metaphors. Participant-directed processing has several advantages. Instead of funneling through a conversation of "What?" "So what?" "And now what?" from the lens of the facilitator, participants describe the connections they see between their experience and their daily life. Because it is more open ended, participants may move processing into unexpected but useful directions; more importantly, participants begin to process on their own. Consider starting with participant-directed methods before moving to large-group question-and-answer sessions if reflecting and processing are new to your participants.

The last step, **independent reflection**, requires the least amount of facilitator guidance. However, it relies on optimal participant engagement. This engagement can be encouraged by establishing a tone and a location that are conducive to a reflective mood and a commitment by the participants to make the experience significant. Participants who are prepared for independent reflection have the necessary foundation to see the meaning in their experiences and the skills and motivation to process on their own.

Alternative Processing Themes and Questions

With practice, facilitators can begin to recognize what direction to take a debrief while the activity is still in process. With a keen eye and a sharp ear, a facilitator will recognize the subtle shifts of a group's dynamics that are the potential launching pads for meaningful discussion. The questions listed below may help you change direction when you notice your group learning something unanticipated during an activity.

Challenge
- What were some challenges that the group faced and how did you deal with them?
- How does a person's attitude affect their ability to overcome challenges?
- What are some necessary skills to utilize when working to overcome challenges?
- Which skill did you practice today that you might use to overcome a challenge tomorrow?

Communication
- Which communication skills were necessary to solve the problem?
- Were there any breakdowns in the group's communication? If so, what were they and how did they affect the outcome?
- What makes communication such an important skill for working cooperatively with a group?
- Which communication skill are you going to work on improving?

Giving and Receiving Help
- What does it take to receive help from someone else?
- Who gave help to someone else? How did it help?
- What are different ways people can help each other?
- How does being a helper improve your community?

Kindness
- Who demonstrated kindness during this activity?
- How does being kind make you feel?
- Why is kindness important on a team?
- How do you demonstrate kindness every day?

Leadership
- Who demonstrated leadership qualities during this activity?
- What are some qualities of an effective leader?
- Did the group have a leader during the activity?
- How can teammates help a leader to be effective?

Pace
- Did the group rush through the challenge?
- How does speed affect the performance of a team?
- What are the benefits of going slowly? Quickly?
- How does a time limit or deadline affect your performance on a task?

Planning
- Did you all have a plan?
- Did everyone know the plan?
- Did everyone agree with the plan? What are the challenges to developing a plan that everyone can agree to?
- What strategies can you use to stay on track as a team?

Respect
- What are ways we can show respect for other people?
- Did anyone show respect during the activity? How?
- What makes it hard for people to respect others?
- What is one thing you can do to demonstrate your respect for someone different from you?

Risk Taking
- What does it mean to take a healthy risk?
- What is the value in taking healthy risks?
- What are some of the risks people took within the challenge?
- What are some risks that you take every day? Are they healthy risks? Why or why not?

Teamwork
- What are three important ingredients when working together as a team?
- What is challenging about working as a team?
- How did working as a team help the group overcome the challenge?
- What did you learn while working through the challenge as a team?

Trust
- What are the key ingredients in building trust?
- How do you know when you can trust yourself?
- How do you know when someone can trust you?
- What makes trust such an important aspect of working cooperatively with others?

Truth
- What is difficult about telling the truth?
- Have you ever felt relieved after telling the truth?
- How does being honest help groups function more effectively?
- What does "Honesty is the best policy" mean to you?

Processing Strategies

The following are alternatives to large-group question-and-answer process-ing sessions sitting in a circle. While a few are more facilitator directed, such as the Moving Debrief or the Processing Cube, most are participant directed, inviting self-relevant metaphor and analogies. The processing strategies Three Pictures and Pair and Solo Reflective Writing are the closest to true independent reflection.

Active Listening: Participants sit in a circle. While you tell the story of what happened during an activity, participants nonverbally show how involved they felt by gesturing or using facial expressions. Invite others to help with the storytelling if you need it.

Add-On Stuff Sack: On a daylong expedition or series of activities, ask the group to add a memento from the activity to a box, bag, or stuff sack. At the end of the day, unpack the collecting container and use the items to talk about the experience.

Body Part Debrief: Use body part cards or objects and have the group toss the different body parts around the circle. When a participant receives a certain body part, ask them to describe something that happened to them that day that the body part represents.

Bulls-Eye: Ask the group to stand in a circle and identify three group goals. Use a prop to represent each goal. Place the first object, representing the first goal, in the middle of the circle. Ask participants to step forward into the cir-cle to indicate how much effort they made toward that goal during the activ-ity. If they made no effort (0%), they should stay where they are; if they put all of their effort (100%) into the goal, they should move to the center. After participants move, ask for observations and any feedback or corrections. ("Do you think anyone should have placed themselves differently?") Repeat for Goals 2 and 3.

Carabiner Connections: Encourage participants to compare their experiences to a carabiner. This closure experience has several valuable features. It takes advantage of the parallels between a carabiner's function and a participant's function as a group member. For example, carabiners are strong when they are closed: they keep the climber safe and connected to a rope (lifeline) and another person. But when carabiners are open, they are vulnerable. You could use many different objects for this activity. We use a carabiner at KWE because it is part of our natural habitat.

175

Community Puzzle: Each participant colors a piece of a puzzle in response to a prompt about the day or activity. After everyone is finished coloring, each participant tells the group about what they drew or wrote and then adds their piece to the puzzle.

Deck of Cards Debrief: Designate a meaning to each suit within the deck of cards. For example, hearts could represent successes, spades could represent situations that individuals had a difficult time with, diamonds could represent something they noticed about themselves, and clubs could represent something they noticed about another group member. Deal at least four cards per person. Participants respond to its prompt as they play a card.

Domino Debrief: Give each participant a domino. Ask a question about the activity and have each person find a partner who has similar numbers on their domino, or a person who has a domino with numbers that, when added to the partner's, equal the same amount. When everyone is in pairs, participants share their answers to the question with their partners.

Fist of Five: Rate the experience from 0 (a fist) to 5 (all five fingers extended). Ask participants to rate their energy, their involvement, their behavior, the group effort, etc.

Free Association: Ask participants to share answers or responses to questions on sticky notes or scrap paper, then read aloud and sort into themes.

Goals in a Stuff Sack: After the group decides their goals, write them down and put them in a box, bag, or stuff sack. Bring them wherever the group goes and check in on them as needed.

Headlines/Hashtags: Small groups are given a sheet of large paper and markers. Each group writes a headline or hashtag that describes the activity.

I See You: Participants sit or lie in a circle with their heads down. At the count of three, all participants look up to stare at another participant. When two people meet eyes, each has to describe what the other did during the last activity.

Image Cards or Feelings Cards: This debrief allows participants to express their feelings. Spread the cards out in front of the group and have them pick a card that best represents an experience or a feeling that they have had. Ask each participant to share why the card they picked represents them or their experience.

Index Card Castles: This processing strategy is great for large-group debriefs. Divide participants into small groups and give each group a stack of index cards. Participants write different things they learned throughout the day or activity on each card. Each group then builds a castle with their index cards and must connect their castle with at least two other castles.

Key Consensus: Collect a variety of different-looking keys. Assign a metaphor to each key and talk about them at each activity. At the end of the program, give each participant a blank key and encourage them to create their own experiences and metaphors.

Knot Around, Feeling Knotty, Knot Feelings: Tie the two ends of a rope into a knot. Ask the group to stand or sit in a circle. Whoever has the knot can share a thought, experience, compliment, etc. The facilitator determines what can or should be shared when the knot is received for each round. For instance, "When you have the knot, share a highlight or lowlight from the activity" or "When you stop the knot, share something you learned that you should not do during this activity."

Knot Race: Tie two ends of a large rope together with a knot. Then tie two more knots in the rope. Color-code the knots with bandannas, ribbon, flagging, etc. Participants shuffle the rope around the circle until you say stop. The person with the designated color knot asks a question of the other two people holding knots.

Moving Debrief: The group stands in a line or circle. Ask participants to move two steps forward if they agree with your statement. Ask them to take two steps back if they disagree with your statement. This gets the participants physically involved while they reflect and is great for groups that need a lot of movement. For instance, step forward if you feel that you were listened to during the activity and step backward if you feel you were not listened to. Alternatively, move toward the water if you felt calm and present during the activity and move toward the trees if you felt frustrated or out of place.

Pair and Solo Reflective Writing: Ask participants to answer a question with a partner or alone in a journal.

Paper Strengths: The facilitator prepares a certificate for each participant and distributes among the group. Each participant gives a certificate to a peer and receives one back. The participants also exchange compliments or words of encouragement during the exchange.

Partner Interview: Participants interview each other according to a prompt or question.

Playdough: Participants sculpt their response to the experience in clay or playdough and share their sculptures with the group.

Pocket Medic Debrief: Lay out all the supplies from a small first aid kit. Explain what each piece is and what it is used for. Ask the participants to be thinking about which items might represent similarities to themselves as you explain each item. After you are finished explaining, ask each participant to share which item is similar to themselves and why.

Positive Stuffed Animals: When you see someone doing something positive, give them a specific stuffed animal to symbolize the success. They are responsible for passing the creature along to another person when they see a positive attribute in them. This can happen on a regular schedule or serendipitously. At KWE, we had a Mojo Moose for a while.

Postcards: Dig out all of your old postcards and use those the same way that you would use Metaphor Cards. Some postcard companies will donate these to your cause.

Processing Cube: This colorful cube has clear vinyl windows on each side. Slip processing questions into each window and toss the ball around the circle. The recipient answers the question that lands faceup.

Sentence Completion:
I'm really glad that I …
This experience will help me …
I felt good when I …
I surprised myself when I …
I liked …
I disliked …
Today, I was frustrated when …
I never thought I could …
What I learned today is …
Someday I'd like to …
It's hard for me to …
This week I'd like to work on …

Three Pictures: Ask participants to picture three moments. For instance, Picture 1 is something you said or did, Picture 2 is something another person said or did, and Picture 3 shows a magic/good moment for the whole group. Provide a generous pause after describing each picture moment to really allow time for reflection.

Thumbs Up: Ask a series of yes, no, and maybe questions. Every member of the group must give an answer with their thumb (up = yes, down = no, middle = maybe).

Toolbox/Treasure Chest: Before working with your group, compile a treasure chest of random items. Add to it whenever you see something special. When you need a prompted reflection, spread the items out before a group. Let individuals pick up items that metaphorically represent an experience they had during the activity/day/program and then share them with the group. Sometimes it is more fun and less intimidating for participants to do this with a partner or small group.

Tweener Ball: Have the group get into a Magnetic Circle (p. 186). Explain that the object of the game is to not let the ball go in between your legs. If it does, the rest of the group shouts "GOOOOALLL" while you run to get it. When you return, you tell the group something that you liked about the day, such as an activity that you enjoyed or a goal that you met. You then serve the ball back into the group. If the ball goes in between you and another person, you and that person race to go get it. The person who doesn't get the ball will then say something nice about the person who retrieved the ball. The person who retrieved the ball then serves and play continues.

Whip Around: Have participants sit or stand in a circle. Each person shares one word that describes their experience of the activity. This is a very fast debrief technique.

Additional Resources

Materials: Building Your Game Bag

Most of the activities in this book can be facilitated with the reusable, inexpensive materials listed below. A few activities require purchasing single-use materials like T-shirts or building props.

Aluminum foil

Balls (assorted—beach balls, tennis balls, golf balls, etc.)

Basins and bowls of various sizes

Boundary ropes (20 to 30 feet long)

Buckets or large cans

Bull ring: Created by attaching 18 to 24 inch lengths of string to a 2 inch metal or plastic ring; there should be as many lengths of string on each ring as you have participants in the group

Blindfolds or bandannas

Chalk

Chenille stems

Clay or playdough

Crayons

Dice (at least five)

Dominoes

Easel pad

Envelopes

Fabric markers

Feelings Cards: Make your own or cut out the individual cards from the template at the back of the book. Decorate and laminate them for repeated use. (Thanks to Sam Mengual, KWE educator, for illustrating the templates.)

FFEACH Cards: Make your own or cut out the individual cards from the template at the back of the book. Decorate and laminate them for repeated use. (Thanks to Sam Mengual for illustrating the cards.)

Felt (8 x 12 inch variety pack)

First aid kit

Hats

Image Cards: Ubuntu Cards, Climer Cards, or Chiji Cards are our favorites. You can also use photographs, postcards, or magazine pages.

Keys of different shapes and sizes

Kickboards

Marbles

Markers

Masking tape

Name tags

Newspaper

Paper of various kinds and sizes (large easel paper, poster board, 8½ by 11 inch sheets, scrap, sticky notes, index cards, etc.)

Paper plates

Pens and pencils

Pipeline set: One piece of ½ inch (diameter) PVC pipe for each participant (12 inches long, cut in half lengthwise)

Playing cards

Processing cube

PVC pipe or tent pole: ½ inch (diameter) by 10 feet (length)

Racoon circle: These are constructed with approximately 15 feet of 1 inch tubular webbing (the kind that is often used for rock climbing). Tie the webbing into a large loop using a water knot, which is made by tying an overhand knot in one end of the webbing, then retracing that knot with the other end so that, once finished, the ends are facing in opposite directions.

Rope

Scrabble set made from wooden building blocks (details on p. 236)

Skittles

Spot markers

String

Tarp or heavy blanket (4 x 6 feet)

Toothpicks

Tossable objects (foam balls, Beanie Babies, yarn balls, etc.)

T-shirts that can be marked on

Watch

Whiteboard

Wooden building blocks

Xerox Cards: Cut out the individual cards from the template at the back of the book. Laminate them for repeated use.

Organizing Strategies

If you need to divide a group into pairs, try one of these quick sorting activities.

Concentric Circles: Have the group form an inner circle and outer circle of the same size. On the count of 3, the inner circle rotates clockwise and the outer circle rotates counterclockwise. When the facilitator says "Stop," the facing participants are partners.

Find Someone Who … has the same thumb size as you, was born in a different season from you, etc.

Finding "Twins": Decide ahead of time on a category, such as animals, famous people, occupations, emotions, sports, etc. Prepare slips of paper with specific examples of the category you have chosen. Make two slips for each example (one set of three if your group is an odd number). After distributing the slips, each person makes a noise and/or performs a movement associated with the example. The group circulates until all partners have been found.

First Names: Everyone counts the number of letters in their first name and finds someone who has the same number of letters. They are now partners. If a person can't find someone, they can use another name or nickname they are called by (for example, a participant named Matthew may use the name Matt and then look for someone with four letters instead of seven). If they still can't find someone, they can pair up with a person who has the closest number of letters.

Hat Partners: Put a hat in the middle of the circle. Ask everyone to look at the hat. Quickly, the leader says "People." Each person looks up at someone else in the circle. If eye contact is made with the other person, the two people are a pair and leave the circle. If eye contact is not made, there is no match. The leader quickly calls out "Hat" and the group members focus their eyes on the hat. Activity continues until all members have a partner.

Hop Along: Ask people to hop on one foot. Hop over to another person who is hopping on the same foot.

If you need to divide participants into small groups, try one of these activities.

Arm/Finger Cross: Ask everyone to cross their arms across their chest. It almost always works out that about 50% of participants cross right over left, and the other 50% cross left over right.

Blue Sky: When you say "Blue Sky," participants hold up one to ten fingers. When you say "Green fields, red earth, blue sky. Go!" participants holding up an even number of fingers are in one group, and those holding up an odd number of fingers are in another group.

Commonalities: Quickly make a series of statements and ask participants to raise their hand if this is true of them. The first two people to raise their hands are partners and do not respond to any more statements. In the case of ties, move on to the next question. Sample statements include: My favorite color is red; I am a Pisces; I am a basketball fan; I have blue eyes; etc.

Cries of Animals: Write animal names (cow, cat, pig, etc.) on slips of paper. Write as many of the same animals as you need groups. Distribute one slip of paper to each participant. Participants should not show their slip to another person. Participants need to make the sound of the animal that is written on their slip and listen to the sounds of others in order to form a family of the same animal.

Form a Band: Each band must have a drummer, guitar player, keyboard player, and singer. Each band mimes a performance, complete with air instrumentation, until all of the drummers are in one group, all singers in another, etc. You can create as many band members as you need groups. (The above example gets you four groups.) Similarly, you can do the same with a baseball team (or any other sport). Building teams with pitchers, catchers, hitters, outfielders, and hot dog vendors will generate five groups.

Line Ups: The group lines up according to any variable. Some examples include: oldest to youngest, tallest to shortest, alphabetically by first or last name, chronologically by month and date of birthday. (If you want to add challenge to the process, do not allow people to talk.) Then fold the line in half. The person they are facing is now their partner.

Opposites Attract: Ask each person to pair up with someone who is different from them physically in some way. Examples could include: tall/short, blond/brunette, blue eyes/brown eyes, etc.

Partners by Math: Participants count off. Your partner is the person who adds to your number to make the total number in the group plus one. So if the group has ten participants, each pair needs to add to 11. With an odd-numbered group, there will be one participant left out. Let them choose a pair to join.

Pick a Number: Ask everyone to pick a number between 1 and the number of the size of your group. Those who have picked the same number become partners. If only one person chooses a particular number, ask them to choose another number.

Picture Puzzles: Cut pictures from a magazine so there are half as many pictures as members of the group. If you are working with a theme, try to find pictures related to the theme. Cut each picture in half and mix them up in a hat. Each person takes one piece. Partners are those whose pieces form a complete picture.

Playing Cards: Decide how many groups you want and what size. For example, if you would like to have five groups of five and you want to randomly put them into groups, get five kings, five aces, five twos, five jacks, and five queens (of course, you will need more than one deck of cards) and shuffle them. Pass them out and then group together the five who get the same card.

Thumb Divide: Ask participants to clasp their hands together, thumbs interlocking. If the right thumb is on top, participants are in one group. If the left thumb is on top, they are in the other group.

Using Image Cards: Pass out image cards. Ask participants to pair up by similar or opposite images.

Values Clarification: Present the group with a value statement related to the theme of the day. Ask them to arrange themselves in a line from "Strongly agree" to "Strongly disagree." Encourage discussion so each person is sure they are in the right place in line. Count off by 2s for diverse groups or divide in half for more homogeneous groups.

If you need participants to stand in a circle, let them know what kind of circle.

Magnetic Circle: Feet touching the feet of the individual standing on either side.

Chicken Noodle: Participants stand shoulder to shoulder in a small circle.

Chicken Wing: Participants place their hands on their hips with elbows out as they imagine having chicken wings. Participants touch elbows around the circle to make a medium circle.

Chicken in Flight: Participants spread out for this large circle by stretching their arms out wide, standing on one foot, and leaning over like a chicken flying through the air. This is the largest circle.

Free-Range Chicken: Everyone finds their own spot in the room, sticks their hands straight out to their sides, and spins in a circle. If they have enough room to spin without touching another person, they are a free-range chicken.

The Great Chicken Turnabout: Everyone stands in a Chicken Wing circle. At the count of 3, everyone turns around and faces the outside of the circle.

Creative ways to encourage a group into a circle:
- Time how long it takes to get in the circle.
- Ask the group to form a circle around an object.
- Have participants line up by birthday in the circle.
- Ask participants to gather around a rope loop.

Appendix A: Activities

Alphabetically by Title

By Materials Available

By Group Size

By Space Available

Classroom

Outdoors/Large Open Space

By Major Theme
(Activities are listed from least challenging to most challenging.)

Communication
Simply Paper 24
Sound Maps 26
The Wright Family 78
Line-Ups 82
Told by Fold 126
Xerox 84
Mirage 135
Claytionary 89
FFEACH—Feelings Charades 124
Two on a Crayon 93
Robot 62
Paper Airplanes 120
Peanut Butter and Jelly Sandwich 67
Squiggle Lines 94
Scrabble 96
Eyes, Mouth, Body 87

Goal Setting
Don't Break the Ice 48
Warp Speed 60
Don't Sink the Boat 50
Inchworm 145
My Life Brainstorm 52
Lifelines 164
Moon Ball 64
In a Hat 59
Pass the Can 169
Steal the Bacon 148
How High? 158

Relationship Building
Categories 112
Find a New Spot 116
Is This Seat Taken? 18
That Person Over There 142
Commonalities 122
Card Prediction 16
Poker Face 130
Peek-a-Who? 118
Living Name Tags 114
Community Maps 132
Bodyguard 128

Teamwork
Hula Hoop Pass 140
Gimme That 22
The "Leader" Ship 39
Knots 20
Stepping Stones 150
Bird's Nest 136
Bull Ring 102
Cooperative Tarp 34
Helium Stick 106
Racoon Circles 108

Problem Solving
Ice Cube Exercise 54
Blind Tree Find 56
Group Juggle 146
1, 2, 3 = 20 (Turnstile) 91
Blind Maze 98
The Maze 152
Skittles in a Jar 100
Cooperation Puzzle 105
Over Under Through 161
Peace Treaty 167
Key Punch 68
Human Mastermind 70
Pipeline 74
Tower of Feetsa 156
Traffic Jam 72

Review or Reflection
Autobiographical Poem 31
Play a Card 28
Tap Someone Who 40
How Did We Do Bingo 43
Personal Coat of Arms 32
Inside-Out T-Shirts 36
My Life Brainstorm 52
Letter to Self 45

Appendix B: Templates

Autobiographical Poem

Write a poem about yourself by completing the sequence of sentences below.

My first name: _____

I am ... _____
(four positive words that describe me)

My family is ... _____ _____ _____ _____
(four positive words that describe my family)

I love ... _____ _____ _____ _____

I need ... _____

I give ... _____

I fear ... _____

I would like to be ... _____

I would like to see ... _____

I wonder ... _____

My last name: _____

194

Bingo Card

B	I	N	G	O
Laughed	Offered a suggestion	Developed a new skill	Talked to someone new	Listened to someone
Used my problem	Said "Thank you"	Was glad to be part of this team	Tried something new	Helped someone
Saw something surprising	Cheered someone on	Considered a different point of view	Made an improvement	Sacrificed my goals for the good of the group
Tried but just couldn't	Played outside my comfort zone	Applauded	Learned something new	Played a different role
Felt challenged	Felt confused	Asked someone for help	Said "I am sorry"	Changed something

Coat of Arms

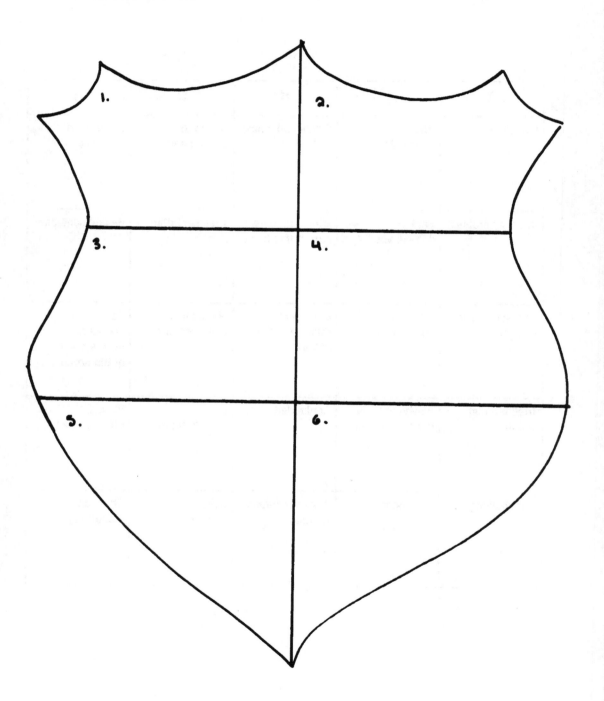

Cooperation Puzzle

Making the puzzles: Copy the puzzle below onto poster board or other suitable material. Each group of four participants will need five puzzles. Make each group's puzzles all the same color (this makes it more challenging). Mix the pieces of the five puzzles together and distribute them among four envelopes. Repeat for as many groups as you will have. (Mark each set of envelopes, so you know which four envelopes go together!)

nervous

CONFUSED

DISAPPOINTED

LONELY

201

202

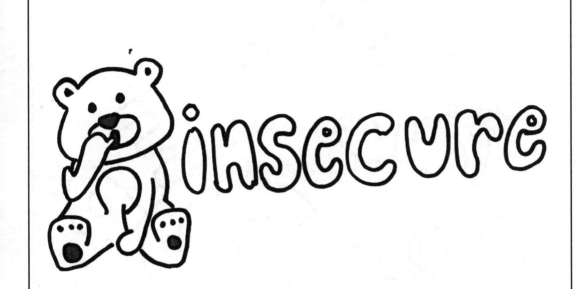

FFEACH Cards

microwave

OVEN

224

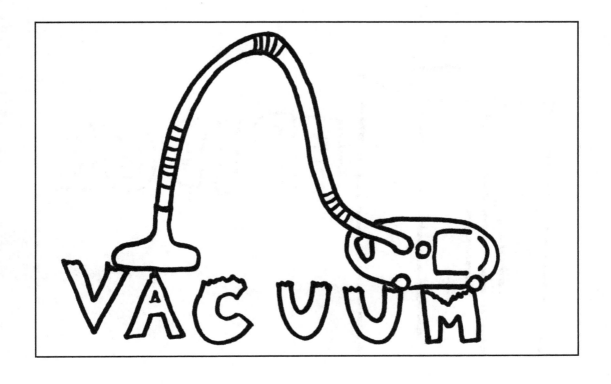

VACUUM

ELECTRIC TOOTHBRUSH

231

232

My Life Worksheet

Answer the following questions. You can use complete sentences or simply list the answers.

What do I enjoy doing?

What are my talents and skills?

Who do I admire? Why?
(List at least three people. They can be people you know personally or people you've heard about in history or the media.)

If I return for a high school reunion many years in the future, what are five things I hope to have accomplished?

How would I like my friends to describe me?
(Identify at least three qualities.)

Scrabble Set

Letter	Frequency	Value
A	9	1
B	2	3
C	2	3
D	4	2
E	12	1
F	2	4
G	3	2
H	2	4
I	9	1
J	1	8
K	1	5
L	4	1
M	2	3
N	6	1
O	8	1
P	2	3
Q	1	10
R	6	1
S	4	1
T	6	1
U	4	1
V	2	4
W	2	4
X	1	8
Y	2	4
Z	1	1
Blank	2	0

T-Shirt Template

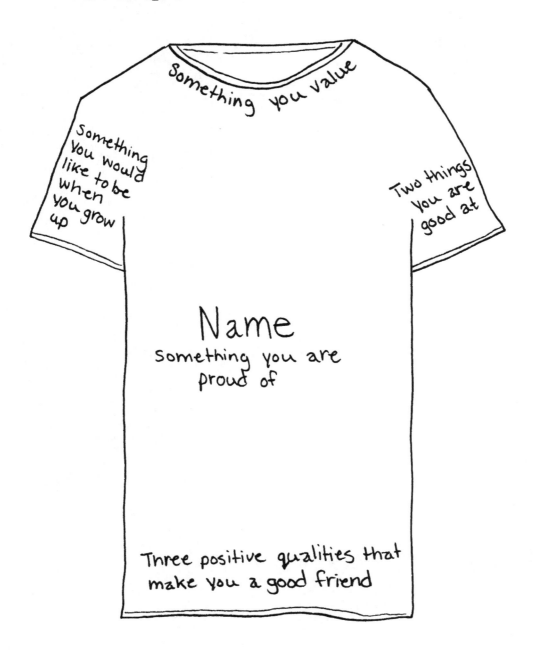

Something you value

Something you would like to be when you grow up

Two things you are good at

Name
something you are proud of

Three positive qualities that make you a good friend

Xerox Images

240

241

Find

keep

in

out

17

243

About Kieve Wavus Education

Camp Kieve was founded as a summer camp in 1926 by Donald Kennedy, a Philadelphia teacher with a heart to reach the underserved children of rural and impoverished areas. The Kennedy family ran Camp Kieve, a summer camp for boys, from 1926 to 1974.

In 1974, the family business was incorporated as a nonprofit organization, Kieve Affective Education, to create new opportunities for reaching more young people and to provide programming for children most in need of the opportunities, virtues, and skills that the organization had grown to embody.

Over the next three decades, the organization developed multiple programs that allowed it to reach more and more children over longer periods of time, slowly renovating the seasonal campus into a year-round facility capable of comfortably accommodating up to 250 young people. A merger with the Wavus Foundation in 2005 created a new organization, Kieve Wavus Education Inc., and further expanded the organization's capacity and commitment to providing life-shaping opportunities to young people and adults.

Today, Kieve Wavus Education serves more than 10,000 young people and hundreds of adults annually through dozens of retreats and programs.

Find out more by visiting www.kwe.org, emailing info@kwe.org, or calling (207) 563-5172.

CPSIA information can be obtained
at www.ICGtesting.com
Printed in the USA
LVHW010815050820
662367LV00006B/74